CATCH 2014

WHY 'YES' LOST THE REFERENDUM, AND WHY, IF WE'RE NOT CAREFUL, WE MIGHT END UP DOING IT AGAIN

Thanks to Kirsty MacDonald, Carolyn Scott, Christopher Silver, James Devoy and the family Foster. Special thanks to Maggie Chapman. Proofread by Chris Foster.

www.jack-foster.co.uk
www.twitter.com/jackfostr

First Edition: January 2019

Jack Foster is a political journalist and documentary film-maker, originally from the Scottish Borders. During the 2014 referendum on Scottish independence, he directed the feature-length documentary *Scotland Yet* and was one of the presenters of the satirical news-spoof *Dateline Scotland*. In 2015, he was a co-creator of the online Scottish Politics radio programme *NewsShaft*.

This book is dedicated to the five per cent.

CONTENTS

THE BELLY OF THE BEAST   16

SURRENDERING THE NARRATIVE   32

THE FOURTH ESTATE   49

MONEY TALKS   69

THE GHOST AT THE FEAST   77

BETTER TOGETHER AND THE "GREY" VOTE   92

THE FORCES OF NATIONALISM   103

THE FEAR FACTOR   111

EYES AHEAD   121

FOREWORD
BY MAGGIE CHAPMAN

In *Catch-2014*, Jack Foster argues that the Yes movement was "the most open, progressive, internationalist
movement that Scotland has ever seen". I agree. The run
up to the 2014 Scottish Independence Referendum saw
some of the most invigorating, ambitious and hopeful
political activism many of us had ever experienced.

I first met Jack in and around the independence campaign: I became familiar with his work as a journalist who sought to promote alternative media and open
up the space for different voices to be heard, different
stories to be told. His involvement in projects such as
Scotland Yet, Dateline Scotland, and, post-referendum,
NewsShaft, solidified his reputation in my, and others'
opinion, as a diligent, thoughtful and empathetic political journalist, with a knack for cutting through the crap
that is so often spewed out onto our airwaves and into
our print media. And yet, as he so eloquently details in
Catch-2014, such analysis and insight is seldom valued
by the Scottish media, never mind the political class, as
a whole.

And this is one of the reasons why *Catch-2014* is an
important book. I hope people who voted No in 2014
will read this book. I hope the most ardent Unionists
will read this book. I hope those who have always been,
and will always be Independence supporters will read

this book. Because there are lessons for all of us to learn from what happened in the run up to and in the immediate aftermath of 18 September 2014.

Reading it reminded me of how angry I am – and should be – at our current political state: democracy desperately in need of reinvigoration and politics calling out for diversity of representation and participation. But reading it also reminded me of the vital role that hope and optimism should play in our politics. It is easy to forget this, especially in the face of defeat and loss.

Most, if not all, political campaigns are characterised, to some degree, by loss: loss as a consequence of not winning enough votes; loss as in the grief of defeat; loss as one's dreams of something different – something better – are shattered. And all sides (because it was not just Yes and No, no matter what we might have been told to believe) of the 2014 vote lost something as the results of the referendum began to trickle and then rush in in the early hours of Friday 19 September 2014.

Catch-2014 uses the lens of the loss faced by the Yes campaign to analyse the roles the media, corporate power, political parties and the institutions of the state played in the 45% to 55% vote share for Yes and No. No won the vote but lost the campaign. Yes won the campaign but lost the vote. This enduring feature of the 2014 campaign underpins what many of us think: Scottish Independence is inevitable, but the timing of this remains uncertain and contested.

The scene setting of Chapter 1, "The Belly of the Beast", rightly credits the SNP for creating the opportunity for the Referendum, whether or not it was ready for it. The system by which we elect the Scottish Parliament has been known to produce some weird and wacky outcomes, from the rainbow parliament with its Green, Socialist and independent groups in 2003, to the SNP majority government – something that was never meant to happen – in 2011. The introductory analysis also high-lights two important features of Scottish politics. Firstly, it is clear from Iain Gray's 2010 comments about the Scottish Labour Party being more than a party – being a movement – that Scottish Labour had both identified the role they should be playing in Scotland, but also that the party was incapable of understanding how to do this. It seems, eight years on, that this is still a difficult lesson to learn. And secondly, in a similar vein, Jack very clearly outlines the very real damage that the partisan approach to the Yes campaign has done to what was, and is, a plu-ralist movement. Again, a lesson we would all do well to remember.

Jack extends this theme of political turf abandoned and opportunities foregone in Chapter 2, "Surrendering the Narrative". Better Together, the No campaign, took and maintained control of the parameters of the debate. The Yes campaign was swamped by challenges and questions that Jack identifies as complete red herrings. The irony is certainly not lost on me that the mess that is Brexit in 2018 might have been avoided had Westmin-ster's Conservative Government learnt this lesson prior to the European Referendum of 2016. But that's for an-other book.

What Jack lays out, starkly, in this chapter is the inevitability of defeat when vision and ambition are squashed. Yes Scotland's "status quo but better" future around currency, around energy, around pensions, and so much more, was not exciting. The vision and radical agenda of the Radical Independence Campaign, Green Yes, and others, were what excited people, and started to lift support for independence above the 30% mark.

The role played by the media cannot be underesti-mated, as discussed in Chapter 3, "The Fourth Estate". Not because the media was necessarily biased or against Yes (although Jack acutely identifies the damage done by the media in demonising online Yes campaigners), but because it is clear that the Scottish media failed (and I think still does fail) to do its job properly: that is, to reflect the country it is there to inform. Just as very little media reflected what 45% of Scotland thought, so the grassroots and community activities and groups that make up so much of our social interactions and lives were pretty much uniformly ignored. No matter what your thoughts on independence, this should concern us all. Our journalism needs a very big shake-up if the media of the future is to do the job required of it effectively.

We live in a capitalist world. It is small wonder, then, that the wealthy tend to have more power. Not only was this power reflected in the way the media reported and analysed Scottish politics at the time, it was also manifested in the way in which big business wielded influence for the status quo. "Money Talks", Chapter 4, describes how corporate interests swayed opinion, with next to no challenge from those that should have done better.

Having touched on it earlier, Chapter 5, "The Ghost at the Feast" discusses the gaping hole in Scottish politics left by a moribund Scottish Labour Party, both prior to and following referendum day. But Jack does so sympathetically, and perhaps more fairly than many of us, who wished Scottish Labour would be an opposition force that challenged and improved the Scottish Government, would have done.

The next two chapters, "Better Together and the 'Grey' Vote", and "The Forces of Nationalism", speak, I think, to two poorly-understood, under-analysed, and yet crucial features of Scottish – and British – politics. Identifying the intergenerational divisions, around willingness to leap into the unknown, around engaging with alternative media, and so on, should have led to a different approach in the EU Referendum campaigns. And the comparison of the very different treatments given to British and Scottish nationalisms should give all of us cause to stop and think how we talk about what is normal, and how we understand boundaries and borders. At a time when young people face worse prospects than their parents for the first time in modern history, and when the fascistic elements of the far right are rearing their heads across Europe, we cannot afford NOT to take these two issues very seriously.

"Project Fear" won the battle for the No campaign. In "The Fear Factor", Chapter 8, Jack discusses just how fear was and can be used as the most powerful of mobilising forces. Again, this is something that should concern all of us with an interest in Scotland's future, regardless of its constitutional state. Where fear is used to cow, disable, and disempower, democracy cannot flourish.

This is perhaps, for me, the overriding message of *Catch-2014:* regardless of our constitutional future, debate, discussion and the teasing out and working through of new ideas is vital for our democracy. People everywhere in the UK – not just in Scotland – are suffering at the hands of the broken institutions of the British state. We desperately need to recapture the energy and enthusiasm for political engagement that was a feature of the Yes campaign. We need to create a media that works for us. We need to learn how to challenge corporate power constructively and robustly. *Catch-2014* brilliantly illustrates these points. And it lays down the challenge to all of us: whatever our political campaigning activity in the future, we must be better at understanding the errors, failings and weaknesses of the past. Otherwise, we are doomed to repeat them.

Maggie Chapman
Co-convener of the Scottish Green Party

INTRODUCTION

Supporters of the Union, those who campaigned for a
No vote in the 2014 Scottish independence referendum,
will argue that this book is unnecessary. They'll say the
reason Yes lost the referendum is simple: *The Scottish
electorate rejected nationalism.* But of course, it was far
more complex than that.

Of the 1.6 million Yes voters, it would be difficult to
find a single individual who was not extremely passionate and motivated about the potential of independence,
or unwilling to share their reasons for backing a Yes
vote.

Yes was a campaign that was comfortable in its own
skin, hopeful for the future and unafraid to shout it loud-
ly from the rooftops. The contrast with those who voted
No could not have been starker.

Unlike their pro-independence counterparts, No voters were characteristically reluctant to be drawn into
conversation about the referendum, often choosing to
keep their voting intentions to themselves. The No vote
is widely regarded – even amongst its most ardent cham-
pions – as one made with reluctance, and a certain degree of resentment.

The reasons for that stark contrast between the behaviour of Yes and No voters are innumerable, but essentially it boiled down to a crucial fact about the unionist vote: it was not – perhaps somewhat ironically – a
united, or coherent group. Unlike the Yes vote, which
comprised a solid, motivated movement, the No cam-

paign relied on a heady mixture of partisan animosity, fear, apathy, disinterest and a subtle, yet potent, dose of British nationalism.

It is likely that only a small proportion of those who voted No did so for genuinely "unionist" reasons. Indeed, many opponents of independence were extremely uncomfortable describing themselves as unionists. Many of them didn't hold any sort of natural affinity with the politics of Westminster, and many wouldn't be seen dead waving a Union flag.

The No vote was in every sense a negative one, yet not so much a rejection of Scottish independence, as it was a rejection of the debate itself.

Those of us who supported the drive for independence in 2014 – and I count myself amongst them – have a tendency to scoff at the "Better Together" campaign and, indeed, at No voters in general. We would do well to remember, however, that Scotland is not yet independent, and despite the seemingly unanimous opinion that it's an inevitability, we do still need to win that independence.

When the next referendum comes around, as it surely will, we cannot simply hope that things will go differently. Who knows? Perhaps they will, but hope alone is a risky strategy, especially given the potentially fatal blow that a second No vote would deal to the independence movement.

There has been a tendency to blame the defeat of 2014 on external factors: a biased media, corruption of the civil service, MI5 infiltration, or – most outlandish of all – brazen vote rigging. Few have been willing to acknowledge the far less fanciful, far more obvious mistakes made by their own side.

For example, hardly anybody wants to consider the major miscalculations made by the Scottish National Party, or the official "Yes Scotland" campaign, which fell far short of the effective, influential campaign it should, and easily could, have been.

A reasonable amount of time has passed since the morning of 19 September 2014, but as the wounds continue to heal, a lot of collective soul searching still needs to be done.

Tempting though it might be to dig out the old banners and rush headlong into another referendum campaign without pause, this is surely the time to ask ourselves some difficult questions. Because if we don't fully understand why we lost the referendum in 2014, what's to stop us doing it all over again?

1

THE BELLY OF THE BEAST

"There's a way of playing safe, there's a way of using tricks and there's the way I like to play which is dangerously, where you're going to take a chance on making mistakes in order to create something you haven't created before."

Dave Brubeck

The winter of 2010 brought with it freezing temperatures and record snowfall across Scotland. But whilst the country negotiated icy pavements, power cuts and snow-filled driveways, a largely forgotten political drama was playing out within Holyrood's corridors of power.

As 2010 drew to a close, Scotland's minority SNP government was at crisis point. Only three years earlier, under Alex Salmond's leadership, the party had made its first major breakthrough. The 2007 SNP victory may have been a narrow one – scraping ahead by just one MSP – but it was a hugely symbolic moment in the party's seventy-three-year history.

The Scottish National Party's transition in status from a perennial party of opposition to that of a credible, electable government had taken a mere eight years since the Scottish Parliament's inception. But after four years at the helm, and with an election looming on the horizon, polling suggested that the electorate seemed far from convinced at the prospect of granting the party a second term in office.

Enjoying a comfortable ten-point lead in the polls, the then Scottish Labour leader Iain Gray looked poised to take back the reins of government, thus ending the Scottish electorate's brief flirtation with the SNP.

Speaking at his party's conference in Oban the same year, buoyed by what seemed like a sure thing, he told delegates:

> *"We had our election failure in 2007. And we learned the lessons. We rediscovered the values which bind us, the purpose which drives us and the vision which calls us. We remembered that we are a movement, not just a party, driven by principle not just a programme. We came out stronger and we are fighting back."*
>
> *Iain Gray MSP (2010)[1]*

It wasn't mere political hyperbole either; everything was pointing towards a comeback for Scottish Labour. Consequently, the mood within the Scottish government, and the SNP at large, was one of defeat. As the sword of Damocles loomed over the party, many of its MSPs were quietly scanning the job market, gritting their teeth at the prospect of what would almost certainly be an embarrassing defeat.

The polls were so heavily in Labour's favour (the gap

was as wide as sixteen points by January) that even die-hard SNP devotees had by this point written off the prospect of anything short of disaster. As one dyed-in-the-wool activist eloquently put it to me at the time: "we're going to get humped".

It wasn't until the end of March 2011 that the polls narrowed to the point at which the SNP and Labour were neck and neck, just six weeks away from the election.

For Scottish Labour to lose a sixteen-point lead might have been described as unprecedented, even careless, but absolutely nobody could have predicted what happened next.

Scottish Parliament FPTP Constituency Vote Polling 2010-2011
(IPSOS-MORI)

On Thursday, 5 May 2011, Scottish voters not only returned the SNP to power, but also increased their share of the vote by such mammoth proportions as to allow them to form a majority government. Such a scenario – as most people are now aware – was previously considered a practical impossibility.

The voting system for the Scottish Parliament had been designed to make it incredibly difficult for any single party to form a majority. More cynical commentators have latterly suggested that this was a ploy, implemented by the Labour Party at the birth of devolution, in order to safeguard against the prospect of potential SNP administrations in the future. If it was such a ploy though, it hadn't worked.

As the results were announced across Scotland that night, it became apparent that something substantial had shifted in Scottish politics. Labour Party frontbenchers fell one after the other as the SNP swept the board – not just in their traditional heartlands, but in every corner of Scotland.

High profile Labour figures like Andy Kerr, Pauline McNeill, Frank McAveety and Des McNulty all lost their seats to the SNP. The Labour leader Iain Gray – following several recounts – managed to hold his East Lothian constituency, but only by the skin of his teeth, with his majority slashed from 2,109 to just 151.

The following afternoon, a victorious but bleary-eyed Alex Salmond spoke to members of the press gathered outside Edinburgh's Prestonfield House Hotel:

> *"When our movement began, it called itself the National Party of Scotland. And that is what it is today again. A party for all the people; a national party."*
>
> *First Minister Alex Salmond (2011)*

That the SNP had scooped a majority of seats in the Scottish Parliament was significant in and of itself, but what made that victory truly historic was what it made possible.

For the first time since the Act of Union in 1707, the Scottish people would be consulted on their continued membership of the United Kingdom; there would now, without doubt, be a referendum on independence.

For Scotland, this was a huge moment, and nothing could – or would – ever be the same again.

Now, I'm sure that most people reading this book will be familiar with what happened in the Scottish election of 2011. Just how unlikely the outcome seemed only a few months beforehand, however, is largely forgotten, and the subsequent impact of that on the SNP is often overlooked in the analysis of what followed.

You see, when a political party enjoys a landslide victory, it has usually planned and strategised towards that moment for years, even decades. But as a result of the runaway success of 2011, the SNP were caught on the hoof, entirely unprepared for the next stage.

*   *   *

The runaway success of the SNP in 2011 has been attributed to a multitude of factors, not least the apparent ineptitude of Scottish Labour, something which only seems to have become more evident in the intervening years (but we'll get to that in Chapter 5).

The SNP's record on tangible policies such as free prescriptions, scrapping Margaret Thatcher's "right-to-buy" scheme and a council tax freeze were popular. Even the normally hostile press got behind Alex Salmond's 2011 campaign. *The Scottish Sun* – which just four years earlier proclaimed "Vote SNP Today and You Put Scotland's Head in the Noose" – ran with the characteristically Murdochesque headline "Play it Again Salm", urging its readers to back the SNP.

Ironically, much of the party's success in 2011 was put down to a perception that it no longer presented any real threat to the UK constitution. Having proved itself as a competent government, even hardened unionists were now comfortable voting SNP, not least because the party itself – or at least its leadership – had pretty much stopped talking about independence.

Of course, the humiliating collapse of the Scottish Liberal Democrats – following their fateful Westminster coalition with the Tories – played a major role in boosting the 2011 SNP vote too. Given the extent to which Lib Dem support had come to capitalise on a widespread disillusionment with the Labour Party, it was only natural that many of those votes should be scooped up by the SNP. More than anything, though, the Lib Dems and the SNP are actually very close to one another politically; the constitutional debate provides the illusion of a gaping ideological chasm between the two parties that simply doesn't exist.

The one thing we do know for certain is that what propelled the SNP towards its majority second term most certainly was not an appetite for Scottish independence.

Polling on the independence question at the time of the election averaged a meagre 28 per cent support for independence, with no sign of a shift on the horizon; all of this despite the huge surge in popularity for the SNP, a party for whom independence was its raison d'être.

Ultimately, it's very easy to forget that the referen-

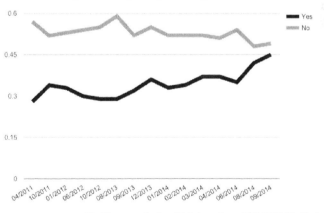

Yes/No support for Scottish independence, 2011-2014 (YouGov)

dum was little more than a fortuitous side effect of the SNP's unexpected landslide, and because of that the party had absolutely no strategy in place regarding its implementation, let alone how it might go about winning.

A significant side effect of the SNP's overnight success was the hasty promotion of a large number of its staffers. Some of the party's high-ranking advisors and strategists began to cultivate carefully crafted narratives of their own, styling themselves as Mandelsonesque figures, whose influence and strategic prowess supposedly lay behind the SNP's success.

In reality, as is so often the case, many of these individuals simply found themselves in the right place at the right time.

The ascendency of the SNP signalled a seismic shift from the established political order, but with that shift came equally seismic changes within the SNP: a party whose base had previously been the sole preserve of hardened activists was for the first time attracting a whole new breed of career politicians.

I recall a conversation I had with a Labour Party advisor in late 2011. He had been asked to lead a colleague's campaign to become a Labour Member of Parliament and had cynically, yet quite earnestly, suggested that they try to get selected as an SNP candidate instead, because "that's the way it's going".

The unexpected landslide of 2011 resulted in a governing party whose benches were now packed with MSPs who were never in a million years intended as anything more than list fodder. Take, for example, the North East MSP Mark McDonald, whose victory was so unexpected that he turned up to the count wearing jeans and a T-shirt.

Furthermore, as the party's group of elected representatives grew to such unwieldy proportions, it was only natural that its unelected team of advisors and strategists should become disproportionately more powerful. After all, the business of ensuring that the party remained a coherent unit, speaking with a united voice, was now more important than ever.

With an independence referendum looming, the safety-conscious approach of the party's faceless, unelected staffers began – understandably – to encroach more and more.

In hindsight, the overt caution which defined those early days might seem a tad misguided, but it's important to remember the context in which the party was operating at the time. It's strange to think, but prior to September 2014, the prospect of a referendum defeat was largely predicted to signal the death of the Scottish National Party, not to mention the relatively dormant independence movement. Given that, the conventional wisdom of the time decreed the need for a delicate balancing act if the party was to emerge unscathed on the other side.

It's one of the worst-kept secrets in Scottish politics that the SNP didn't think an independence referendum winnable from the outset. The referendum wasn't something the SNP had planned and, ironically, it wasn't something they particularly wanted to undertake.

Such a vote presented a huge risk for the party, and so damage limitation had to be a guiding principle from the outset. The approach evolved towards a more cautious optimism as the debate developed, but that initial apprehension would ultimately set the underlying tone of the entire SNP/Scottish government campaign for independence.

*   *   *

On Friday, 25 May 2012, the Cineworld complex at Edinburgh's Fountain Park played host to a glitzy, high profile launch for the official cross-party campaign for independence, entitled Yes Scotland. There were lanyards aplenty, lots of press, the singer Dougie MacLean, actor Brian Cox and more than a few confused cinemagoers.

Representatives from pretty much every political party other than Labour and the Liberal Democrats were in attendance, much to the chagrin of *The Daily Telegraph's* Scottish Editor, Alan Cochrane, who could be heard deriding the small – yet largely forgotten – group of "Conservative Voters for Scottish Independence".

Other than the press, and a select few Green Party or Scottish Socialist Party dignitaries, it soon became apparent that the assembled crowds had been sourced almost exclusively from a mailing list of SNP members. The staff handing out the passes looked visibly embarrassed when I pointed out the slight conflict such a partisan guest list presented for a campaign purporting to be, well, non-partisan.

The event was much maligned by the press, but then it was always likely to be. The controversial Labour hack Iain Smart branded it "The declaration of Cineworld", and just as a stopped clock tells the right time at least twice a day, he did have a point. Large elements of the Yes launch comprised a lot of style but little substance, with what felt a lot like a last-minute, cobbled together cast.

The launch of Yes Scotland was something of a mixed bag, but it set out very clearly the tone with which its architects wished it to operate – and indeed stuck to till the bitter end. A relatively hands-off organisation, it was geared towards branding more than anything else, but essentially it was intended as a bulwark, to protect the SNP from any potentially negative fallout.

Yes Scotland's status as an SNP shield was further reinforced by the appointment of PR "guru" Jennifer Dempsie, a former special advisor to Alex Salmond, at the very heart of the organisation. Whilst Dempsie appeared to have no official position within the campaign – she was not a director, nor was she on the advisory board – it's understood that she wielded considerable influence over day-to-day operations.

Many in the upper echelons of Yes Scotland viewed her as the SNP's "enforcer", and given that practically all of Yes Scotland's budget had to be signed off by the party, that gave her considerable influence in the running of the campaign – arguably more than any of its directors.

The SNP's head of communications Kevin Pringle also became a regular fixture at Yes Scotland, and you could be forgiven for thinking that the extent of crossover between the official campaign and the SNP made it practically impossible to know where one began and the other left off.

There is little question as to whether this uneasy relationship between Yes Scotland and the SNP led to the loss of four of its original team of executive directors: Susan Stewart, Jacqueline Caldwell, Ian Dommett and Stan Blackley. The stranglehold over campaign finances by the SNP reportedly caused deep and irreparable strains within Yes Scotland's Hope Street HQ, which were never really recovered from.

Yes Scotland had turned out to be exactly the thing it was designed not to be: an SNP front, which put the campaign in a strange limbo regarding how it paid for things. On the one hand, Yes Scotland was independent from the SNP, but on the other, it was entirely reliant on its war chest to function. Understandably, the SNP – having spent decades leading the charge towards independence – weren't keen on handing the reins over to someone else. Consequently, the campaign ended up under de facto SNP management, much to the annoyance of former directors like Stan Blackley, who very publicly expressed his frustration at the way in which Yes Scotland had been "captured" by the SNP:

> *"Many will be surprised to learn that Yes Scotland no longer produces its own campaign resources. The Yes-branded newspapers currently dropping through letter boxes are written and produced by the SNP. The only clue to this is the tiny imprint hidden on an inside page. The Yes billboards that have appeared in every town and city in recent weeks were devised by a creative team engaged by the SNP without any input from what remains of the Yes Scotland team, which often only sees these resources well after they've been distributed to SNP members and activists."*
>
> *Stan Blackley (2014)[2]*

At this point, you would be forgiven for asking who on earth could be better placed to run Scotland's first official independence campaign than the Scottish National Party?

Don't get me wrong, the SNP have successfully led the vanguard for independence for the best part of a century, and it was only as a result of their resilience and hard work that the 2014 referendum came about in the first place. For that, the SNP deserve full credit. They had certainly earned the right to lead the campaign if they so desired, but there are convincing arguments as to why that might not have been the savviest approach.

Throughout the lifetime of the SNP – seventy-three years at that point – the party had built a solid base of support for independence, comprising around 30 per cent of the population. That level of support, however, had remained somewhat stagnant for at least a decade or so, and one might argue that if the SNP hadn't convinced you of the merits of independence by that point, it was doubtful they were ever likely to. For this reason more than at any other point in recent history, pro-independence voices from outwith the SNP were crucial.

Instead of trusting that task to others, however, the SNP embarked on a lukewarm campaign to woo its detractors with a strikingly conservative vision of how a post-independence Scotland might look.

Indeed, the Scottish government's strategy with regards the entire independence debate was one of damage limitation: don't scare the horses; nothing too radical; softly, softly, catchee monkey. That strategy wasn't working though. Polling in favour of independence sat at around 30 per cent for the first year of Yes Scotland's official campaign, and it wasn't until the summer of 2013 before support slowly started to shift in favour of Yes.

That shift, however, was not due to Yes Scotland, or the SNP's campaigning prowess; rather it was the beginning of what was to become the independence campaign we all remember.

*　　　　*　　　　*

In May of 2013, the Radical Independence Campaign (RIC) exploded on to Scotland's political landscape following a lively run-in with the right-wing, Eurosceptic UKIP leader Nigel Farage outside an Edinburgh pub. That now infamous confrontation ended with Mr Farage being escorted from the scene by police after two separate taxi drivers refused his custom.[3]

RIC was essentially a loose coalition of left wing, radical political parties and trade unionists, which included the likes of the Scottish Socialist Party, the Scottish Greens and pro-independence elements of Scotland's trade unionist movement. RIC wanted to highlight the possibilities for radical, socialist politics following a Yes vote, and made a name for itself conducting mass canvass events, during which it would descend on the often forgotten housing schemes which lie at the edges of Scotland's major towns and cities. Without doubt, that proactive approach embodied by RIC played a pivotal role in moving the independence campaign from its somewhat woolly, middle-class beginnings, towards the overwhelmingly working-class movement it became.

One of RIC's founders, Cat Boyd, talked of the political awakening she witnessed while canvassing:

> *"A guy answered the door. He was in his fifties … He said: 'You know, no one's been to my door in over a decade to ask what I think.' That's shameful. That is the true failing of British politics."*
>
> *Cat Boyd (2014)[4]*

Radical Independence certainly traces some of its roots to a frustration with the official Yes Scotland campaign, an organisation that many would-be activists found to be faceless and impenetrable. More than once, in those very early days of the campaign, I remember people complaining that they had tried to get involved, but that Yes Scotland simply hadn't responded; I can personally attest to that too.

So, rather than sitting around waiting for the campaign to come to them, they set about launching their own.

From the start, RIC produced its own literature and organised its own events. In essence it was a movement within a movement, and following the success of this style of campaigning, it began to find itself replicated across the country.

Before long, entirely autonomous campaign groups were springing up all over Scotland using online crowd-funders to pay for resources, initiating regular debates, hustings and even dedicated shops and cafes staffed by enthusiastic local volunteers.

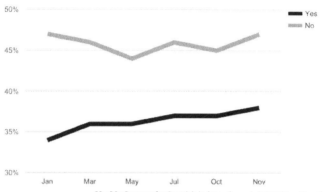

Yes/No Support for Scottish independence in 2013 (Panelbase)

Meanwhile, Yes Scotland seemed to be treading water – hamstrung, as ever, by low morale and SNP budget restraints; the official campaign had essentially become little more than an outlet for Yes-branded key rings and car stickers. Strangest of all, Yes Scotland seemed reluctant – at least to begin with – to align itself in any official capacity with the abundance of new grass roots Yes groups. Except, that is, for the somewhat conservative Business for Scotland and, latterly, National Collective.

The Artists' and Creatives' Collective offered an obvious appeal to the SNP in that its model was very similar to that of Yes Scotland. It looked young, stylish and exciting, but beneath the gloss it offered little in the way of any tangible vision.

Given that several of National Collective's former directors moved pretty much seamlessly into lucrative roles within the Scottish National Party after 2014, it should come as no surprise that regular below-the-radar strategy meetings were held with the SNP throughout the 2014 referendum campaign. Below the radar, of course, because it would have undoubtedly raised eyebrows – given the emphasis National Collective placed on its status as a "non-party" campaign.

Essentially, because the SNP didn't believe a Yes victory was a realistic prospect, it was keen to keep a close eye on the campaign. In fairness though, it was the SNP who stood to lose most, so the desire to maintain full control of the narrative was understandable. That said, they weren't particularly successful in doing that (see Chapter 2).

According to some party insiders, the SNP found itself divided into roughly two camps as the 2014 referendum campaign developed, a division which grew more pronounced in the final months leading up to the vote.

The then First Minister Alex Salmond is understood to have believed wholeheartedly that the Yes campaign could prevail, albeit at the eleventh hour. He was far from alone in that belief, but there were many within the party who didn't share his optimism.

Those who had resigned themselves to the prospect of defeat had started to rally behind the next phase for the party. In essence, they had already left the campaign behind.

That next phase, of course, would be the renewed leadership of Nicola Sturgeon, and the scooping up of the wider Yes movement, freshly galvanised as SNP votes in the wake of a defeat. It is no coincidence that so much of the SNP's energy during the summer of 2014 was focused on aggressively raising Sturgeon's profile, whilst its only tangible offering towards the Yes campaign during those final months was a solitary Alex Salmond touring Scotland giving speeches.

It is odd, to say the least, that every other major political party in Scotland had its own official campaign group during the referendum: United with Labour, Conservative Friends of the Union, Green Yes ... but the official SNP campaign for Yes was notable by its absence.

Perhaps they felt that such a campaign was unnecessary, given the SNP's somewhat obvious support for independence; perhaps it simply didn't dawn on them to set up such a thing. What is more likely, however, is that the SNP were reluctant to plough yet more resources into something they viewed as a lost cause from the outset.

From a party political perspective that strategy certainly paid dividends for them, even if it cost the Yes campaign in the immediate term.

One can't help but wonder, though, had the SNP committed fully to the idea of a Yes victory from the outset, how such a campaign could have developed, and how very different the polls might have looked on 18 September 2014.

SURRENDERING THE NARRATIVE

"The smart way to keep people passive and obedient is to strictly limit the spectrum of acceptable opinion, but allow very lively debate within that spectrum."

Noam Chomsky

On Monday, 25 June 2012, activists and grandees from Scotland's three main unionist parties came together at Edinburgh's Napier University to launch what would become the official cross-party campaign for a No vote in the 2014 independence referendum.

The launch event for the Better Together campaign was a fairly low-key affair, and its centrepiece was a somewhat ghoulish speech by the former Labour Chancellor Alistair Darling:

> *"It is a gamble – a gamble with your jobs, your businesses, your savings. No one advocating change as fundamental as this should*

be afraid of basic questions. And they have a duty to answer them. What are the risks? What are the costs? And ultimately, what is the justification for such division and upheaval? Those who advocate a separate Scotland have had decades to think about the economic fundamentals, yet, in the face of challenge, they are still literally making it up as they go along. They talk about a currency union with what's left of the UK – but haven't thought to ask whether or why anyone else would want this. This is no abstract debate; it's about jobs, and pensions, and the Welfare State, and the survival of businesses."

Alistair Darling (2012)[5]

The essence of Darling's speech would ultimately set the strategic tone for the official No campaign, and Better Together didn't deviate from its message right through to the vote itself.

Better Together, in association with a company called Blue State Digital – the people behind Barack Obama's Web campaigns – realised that the most effective way to bring about a No vote didn't lie in debating the merits – or otherwise – of independence. Rather, the campaign actually went to great lengths to encourage people not to engage with the debate at all.

By presenting an endless list of patently unanswerable questions as a first line of defence, Better Together ensured that they would never be drawn into a genuine debate on independence. Their premise was simple: *until these questions are answered, the argument is moot.*

Of course, questions about the future are inherently unanswerable. Scotland's currency status ten years from now, for example, is no less mysterious than that of the UK's. As Doc Brown says to Marty and Jennifer at the end of *Back to the Future Part III:* "Your future hasn't been written yet, no one's has; your future is whatever you make it."

Doc Brown is, of course, one of the foremost authorities in the world regarding time travel, and Alistair Darling is not. But I'm fairly sure that Darling is capable of wrapping his head around the inherent ambiguities tied up with predicting the future.

Of the 1.6 million people who voted Yes in 2014, it's highly unlikely that many were persuaded to do so because of reassurances over currency; it's probably true to say that membership of the EU played a role, of course, given the massive shift in attitudes towards independence following the Brexit vote in 2016, but independence is first and foremost a matter of principle, and once you support that principle, those questions are exposed for the red herrings they are.

With that in mind, it should have been fairly easy for the Yes campaign to seize the agenda, concentrating on the palpable desire for real change which independence would make possible. Weirdly, though, this is not what happened.

Due to the widespread belief within the SNP and, therefore, by proxy, Yes Scotland, that the referendum was unwinnable, there was no coherent strategy in place for victory. From the very start, Yes Scotland found itself on the back foot, allowing the agenda to be set by Better Together, embarking down a three-year road of persistent, grovelling attempts to answer Alistair Darling's list of impossible questions.

Those "questions" which formed the centrepiece of the Better Together campaign ensured that they would never need to refute the central case for independence: *that the Scottish electorate are better placed to make decisions regarding Scottish affairs than the UK electorate, that of a population outnumbering Scots by nearly 60 million.*

Better Together never needed to form a response to that idea; they would simply say *ah, yes, that's all very well, but what currency will you use?* safe in the knowledge that all responses would, by definition, be speculative and thus unsatisfactory.

But the SNP, the Scottish government and Yes Scotland played into the hands of the Better Together campaign, allowing them to create, manipulate and maintain the narrative that would endure all the way through to 18 September 2014.

Yes Scotland's website actually ended up presenting itself as a dedicated service for answering the so-called "big questions" on independence, but the questions were all written by Better Together. Rather than concentrating on what we might do as a newly independent country, there was a relentless focus on process and the inevitable minutiae tied up in the transition.

*   *   *

On Monday, 25 November 2013, over 200 journalists from every corner of the world gathered at Glasgow's Science Centre as the Scottish government launched its long awaited white paper on independence, entitled *Scotland's Future.*

At a whopping 650 pages long, it promised to conclusively answer any and all questions raised by the prospect of an independent Scotland. On the face of it, the document was impressively extensive, but in many respects it was utterly counterproductive.

Scotland's Future had been devised and written in the face of sustained arguments from opponents over issues such as currency, pensions, Europe and membership of NATO; as such, it read more like a love letter to Better

Together than the blueprint for independence it purported to be.

Alistair Darling must have thought Christmas had come early; not only had the Scottish government chosen to dignify Better Together's surreal and patently unanswerable questions, but they had now set their importance in stone.

From that moment on, the white paper rendered it far more difficult to argue that independence existed as a separate entity from the Scottish National Party, presenting – as it did – a series of party policies on the likes of childcare, pensions and broadcasting as a part of the document.

The blurring of the line between SNP policy and independence was a huge tactical blunder; indeed, if there was a specific moment at which Better Together were effectively handed full control of the referendum's narrative, it was the launch of *Scotland's Future.*

By inserting SNP policy proposals into a document laying out the process for fundamental constitutional change, the white paper performed a pivotal own goal. It completely played into the hands of those who would paint a future independent Scotland – quite disingenuously – as some sort of tartan-clad North Korea, with a dictatorial Alex Salmond at its helm.

In reality, the white paper was a textbook example of overthinking something to the point at which you forget what you were actually trying to achieve in the first place.

What should have consisted of no more than four or five pages somehow ended up as a 650-page tome, large tracts of which could have been drafted by Alistair Darling himself.

It would be incorrect to say that questions about an independent Scotland's economy, its currency and pensions weren't legitimate, but a great deal of misinformation was employed to disguise the fact that, by and large, there wasn't really that much uncertainty.

For example, even the official Better Together campaign never actually claimed that Scotland's economy would flounder in the wake of independence, it merely implied it. In fact, Alistair Darling addressed that very point in his inaugural campaign speech:

> "Our case is not that Scotland cannot survive as a separate state. Of course it could."
>
> *Alistair Darling (2012)[4]*

Likewise, questions surrounding the security of state pension payments were raised constantly, and understandably posed very real, very frightening questions for many Scottish pensioners.

Much like economic sustainability though, the state pension was never in doubt; the UK Pensions Minister Steve Webb even went on record as saying so:

> "Citizenship is irrelevant. It is what you have put into the UK National Insurance system prior to separation."
>
> *Steve Webb MP, UK Pensions Minister (2014)[6]*

Arguably, though, the most divisive issue in the final days of the referendum was that of the currency, wherein a number of respectable politicians and journalists indulged in the idiotic fantasy that an independent Scotland could somehow be barred from using its own money. Furthermore, many unionists gleefully suggested that the rest of the UK might actively refuse to enter into a currency union with a country with which it had been financially integrated for over 300 years.

Those arguments in particular, though, were seen as holding water during the latter stages of the campaign, specifically following a summit between the First Minister and the Governor of the Bank of England, Mark Carney.

Reading the headlines, you'd be forgiven for thinking that Mark Carney had blown the suggestion of a currency union out of the water: "Carney's financial warning raises spectre of crisis" *(The Herald)*; "BoE's Mark Carney reiterates currency union doubts" *(The Scotsman)*; "Salmond takes a Pounding from BoE boss Mark Carney" *(The Sun)*; "Mark Carney hits out at 'incompatible' currency union plans" *(The Telegraph)*.

When you look at what Mark Carney actually said, one wonders whether the headlines were perhaps written before the Governor even opened his mouth:

> "In terms of the financial stability questions – whatever happens in the vote, the Bank of England will continue to be the authority for financial stability for some period of time, certainly over the interim period ... We have responsibilities for financial stability in the United Kingdom, we will continue to discharge those responsibilities until they change. We will continue to discharge those responsibilities regardless of the outcome of the vote on the 18th September."
>
> *Mark Carney, Bank of England Governor (2014)*[7]

All things considered, though, it didn't matter what Mark Carney said to Alex Salmond. The musings of the Governor of the Bank of England are complex, nuanced, and pretty specialist, and as such they tend to go over most people's heads. What that meant was that whichever side had control of the narrative regarding currency at that point in the campaign could claim Carney's comments for themselves – quite regardless of what he had actually said.

If Mark Carney had used the press conference for the sole purpose of demonstrating his ability to moonwalk, it would still have been interpreted as a "blow" to the Yes campaign's case for a currency union, because Yes Scotland had long since surrendered the campaign narrative to its opponents.

Many on the Yes side might well feel frustrated by the way the currency issue was handled, but it's no good getting angry at the Better Together campaign. The reality is, it shouldn't have been possible for a shambolic, disoriented coalition such as Better Together to seize control of the narrative so effectively – but they did, and it's important to understand why they did.

The currency union, like many of the concrete policies to be implemented during the transition to independence, was an SNP idea, and as such the SNP were highly protective over it. In fairness to them, it was probably the most sensible of all the currency plans; the problem is, it was the only one anyone was allowed to talk about.

Early on in the referendum campaign, the SNP effectively placed a moratorium on any discussions around the currency question outwith the established currency union position. Discussions about a separate Scottish currency "pegged" to the rUK pound, for example, were entirely off-limits. By the summer of 2014, a separate Scottish currency was widely acknowledged as being an equally viable option, widely acknowledged by everyone except the SNP and Yes Scotland, who vigorously stuck with the currency union line to the bitter end.

Those strategic decisions were laid down early in the campaign, off the back of a few, largely forgotten, polls suggesting that the electorate were uneasy at the prospect of changing currency. That perceived unease was enough to utterly paralyse the upper echelons of Yes

Scotland, ever-terrified as to how these sorts of "wedge issues" might play out with the ever-elusive undecided voters.

By the same token, Better Together saw from the beginning that they'd been handed the whole currency narrative on a plate, and Yes Scotland's reluctance to discuss other options led to endless and inevitable swipes from its opponents, ranging from thinly veiled racist stereotypes – Irn-Bru bottle tops, Tunnock's Tea Cakes, the Groat, even the Pibroch – to those designed specifically to reinforce the notion that this was all an ego trip by Alex Salmond. Better Together were extremely fond of Photoshopping images of Alex Salmond on to coins; it was, arguably, their favourite trope.

The Director of the Common Weal think tank, Robin McAlpine, wrote in February of 2014 about Scotland's currency options and the dangers of restricting the conversation to that of a sterling union. By that point, though, it was probably already too late to start talking about such things, especially when Yes Scotland would have no part in it:

> "These are decisions we don't need to make right now – but it would almost certainly be better if we had the debate right now. The problem with following polls that say people are nervous about leaving sterling is that it guarantees that they won't hear about the potential benefits of leaving sterling and so their minds will not change even though there are very good arguments that might well persuade them."
>
> *Robin McAlpine (2014)*[8]

Because the Scottish electorate were effectively barred from discussing alternative currency options, those options naturally looked unworkable and risky by the latter stages of the campaign. Alex Salmond's inability to elaborate on a so-called "Plan B" in a televised debate with Alistair Darling was testament to the corner he – and his party – had backed the Yes campaign into. Who could blame Darling for capitalising on that error?

> "Any eight-year-old can tell you the flag of a country, the capital of a country and its currency... I presume the flag is the saltire, I assume our capital will still be Edinburgh, but you can't tell us what currency we will have. What is an eight-year-old going to make of that?"
>
> *Alistair Darling (2014)*[9]

As half of Scotland screamed "the pound!" at their television screens, Alex Salmond was powerless to do anything more than reiterate the Scottish government's currency union line for the umpteenth time. It didn't matter that a currency union was entirely feasible – not to mention in everyone's best interest – but the fact that it hadn't been possible to discuss any alternatives meant that the Better Together campaign had been given free rein to relentlessly attack and discredit the notion for months.

Ultimately, its simplicity became its Achilles' heel. By refusing to acknowledge alternative currency options, Alex Salmond, the SNP and Yes Scotland made it alarmingly easy to be painted as shifty by their opponents. Yet again, the narrative had been utterly surrendered to the opposition, to the point that having a clear and simple position on currency could be – albeit disingenuously – presented as nothing short of evasive, irresponsible propaganda.

Questions regarding EU membership were treated in an almost identical fashion to the currency debate.

Where European leaders remained entirely silent, Better Together projected their own fictitious roadblocks for an independent Scotland's continued membership of the European Union.

Obviously, post-2016, the EU membership argument sticks out most glaringly as a complete nonsense. The oft-pooh-poohed predictions of independence campaigners were, of course, borne out in the terrifying reality of the UK's vote to leave the European Union in June 2016.

Quite how the No campaign was able to get away with peddling that fiction is confusing to say the least: an in/out referendum on EU membership was already on the cards during 2014, and the prospect of the rest of the UK voting to leave was very real. Hindsight is a wonderful thing, certainly, but repudiating informed foresight was very much the order of the day in 2014.

That said, the EU still wasn't a particularly useful argument for the No campaign, given that very few genuinely believed we'd have any issues retaining our membership post-independence – and noises from EU leaders post-Brexit have certainly supported that notion.

Nonetheless, the EU question served as a useful staging post for a pernicious smear campaign whose origins could be found in the following oft-misquoted exchange between Alex Salmond and the BBC's Andrew Neil from 4 March 2012[10]:

> AN: Have you sought advice from your own Scottish law officers in this matter?
>
> AS: We have, yes, in terms of the debate.
>
> AN: And what do they say?
>
> AS: You can read that in the documents that we've put forward, which argue the position that we'd be successor states.

Now, this whole saga is a confusing one, but essentially Salmond's opponents argued that he was flat out lying. They contend that he claimed to have sought legal advice on an independent Scotland joining the EU, a claim that was directly at odds with subsequent revelations that the Scottish government had sought no such advice at that time.

The key phrase from the interview transcript though – and unsurprisingly, the phrase that tended to be edited out when cited by Salmond's detractors – is "in terms of the debate".

Salmond was referring to advice regarding EU membership that had already been sought by the Scottish government, advice that was already in the public domain. It should have come as no surprise that he wouldn't be drawn on the question of further, unpublished advice; it's standard government practice – not just in Scotland, but the UK as a whole – to keep the existence or content of any such thing secret.

Obviously, Salmond's opponents knew all this, but they also knew that most of the electorate probably wouldn't. After all, obscure confidentiality precedents regarding legal advice for a government isn't your standard bedtime reading.

So the Andrew Neil interview became the centrepiece of a campaign to paint Alex Salmond not simply as untrustworthy, but as a proven liar.

It's no coincidence that opponents of the independence campaign went to great lengths from the outset to embody the entire movement in Alex Salmond's likeness. After all, it's far easier to discredit one politician than hundreds of thousands of ordinary Scots.

*　　　*　　　*

As the various examples laid out in this chapter hopefully illustrate, it doesn't really matter what the reality is, or even how obvious that reality might be; if your side has control of the narrative, it can better control the perception of events. If you are still sceptical, don't worry, because I've left the most potent example for last: *North Sea oil.*

During the referendum campaign, I attended hundreds of debates and talks, watched even more videos, read screeds of articles, books and thought-pieces, and I engaged in conversations about independence with people of all ages and backgrounds. What strikes me to this day is that I genuinely don't remember a single occasion where anyone in that wider Yes movement brought up North Sea oil as anything other than a burden to the campaign.

For all its unpredictability and price volatility, there's no question that North Sea oil remained – and remains – the single greatest motivator for the UK to keep Scotland inside the Union. As such, it must exist in a permanent, contradictory state: within the UK, it provides jobs and energy security, but in an independent Scotland, it's a financially volatile terrorist target. It's a paradox that would leave even Erwin Schrödinger scratching his head. The truth, of course, is that it's all those things, regardless of constitutional politics.

One of the fascinating developments of the independence campaign was the extent to which large swathes of the population became hugely informed about issues like energy. You could hardly go from one day to the next without hearing about Scotland's renewable potentials, or more obscure questions about unsatisfactory electricity grid connections from the islands – where wind and wave power is often so plentiful that it could supply the whole of Scotland.

Orkney, for example, is home to some of the leading wave power technology in the world, yet for all the power it generates, the infrastructure to bring it to the mainland simply isn't there.

Yes, these were the sorts of discussions you'd hear on energy at Yes campaign meetings, though you'd never have known it if you took your cues from Better Together:

> "It is absolute madness for the SNP to base their case for separation around a commodity that is declining and volatile."
>
> *Alistair Darling (2013)[11]*

It should be pointed out that whilst that quote appears to be levelled towards the SNP, as opposed to the wider Yes campaign, Better Together made a tactical decision early on to behave as though there was no wider, non-partisan Yes campaign, hence they only ever referred to "the SNP" or "the Nationalists".

According to the Better Together campaign, the case for independence was built entirely on the back of North Sea oil revenue. It wasn't, of course, and Nicola Sturgeon has since conceded that she and her party were perhaps not clear enough about that:

> "So the point here, and it's a point that is often lost about the case for independence, and I take some responsibility for perhaps not getting this argument across strongly enough during the referendum campaign, is that the case for Scotland as a strong independent country was never based on oil."
>
> *Nicola Sturgeon (Andrew Marr Show, Jan 2016)[12]*

To say that the argument was not put across strongly enough is one heck of an understatement. Once again the SNP did neither itself nor the Yes campaign any favours by publishing a weighty section in its white paper, containing forecasts about oil prices. This has since been held up by detractors as the entire funding platform for every single public service in an independent Scotland, and unionists have looked on gleefully as the oil price has fluctuated erratically ever since. We're all meant to share a collective sigh of relief every time we see the oil price drop: *Phew, we dodged a bullet there, didn't we?*

Rarely do we hear about Scotland's potential to provide its citizens with 100 per cent cleaner, cheaper and more reliable renewable energy, our world-renowned tourism sector or Scotland's status as a net exporter of food. We rarely hear about those things, because when the economics of independence get discussed, all anyone seems to want to talk about is the bloody *oil.*

The white paper, though, fanned the flames of the oil reliance myth, and dutifully handed yet another narrative squarely to the Better Together campaign. In fairness to the Scottish government, the white paper was at pains to point out that Scotland's economy was not reliant on North Sea oil. Without oil and gas, the white paper pointed out more than once, GDP per head in Scotland was practically identical to that of the UK as a whole. But the promise to establish a Norwegian style oil fund allowed opponents to paint the plan as either a naïve attempt at a silver bullet to solve all Scotland's financial problems, or a mean-spirited ploy to siphon money away from our English neighbours.

Perhaps a more pernicious problem, though, is the knee-jerk way in which the SNP tend to respond to questions on oil forecasts. Rather than placing them to one side, as mere forecasts, and concentrating on the many other aspects of the Scottish economy – which, without oil, would fare just fine – they have a tendency to start throwing obscure forecast figures back and forth, losing all but the most committed economist by the second or third sentence.

*   *   *

In the end, there was no specific killer blow landed by the Better Together campaign, rather a highly successful ownership of the narrative from the outset. The SNP and Yes Scotland were so nervous that they'd lose the backing of "middle Scotland", that they were lured into the trap of trying to deliver concrete answers to each and every question put forward by the unionist campaign, despite the fact that, more often than not, there just wasn't an answer.

Each and every question posed by Better Together represented a perceived advantage or disadvantage to one or other side in one or other hypothetical post-Yes negotiation. Some were sensible enough – it's perfectly acceptable to want assurances on currency, for example, but many were just filler, illustrated by the widely ridiculed "Better Together's 500 Questions", which included such gems as:

> • What will be the rates for company car taxation?
> • How much would a first class stamp cost in a separate Scotland?
> • What, if any, plans are there for a separate Scottish lottery?
> • What will Scotland's international dialling code be?
>
> *Better Together's "500 Questions" (2014)[13]*

The tactic from the No campaign was to bamboozle people with endless, unanswerable questions, and in fairness, they were pretty good at it. Those of us who were following the campaigns closely could see just how transparent all of that was, but those who weren't – and they were the ones who ultimately swung the vote – found themselves drowning in a sea of seemingly endless complexity and uncertainty.

All of this came together to form the defeatist mantra with which Better Together rallied its supporters, a convenient line which required no follow up, and no effort to justify: *There are just too many unanswered questions!*

Had the SNP believed at the outset that the referendum was winnable, then perhaps a coherent strategy could have emerged to combat Better Together's relentless barrage of contrived uncertainty. But by the time the Scottish government realised what so many others had been saying for years – that a Yes vote *was* possible – it had backed the official campaign into a corner from which there was no escape.

Much has been made since the vote of the triumph of fear over hope. The fear that cost the Yes campaign the referendum, however, emanated initially from the very heart of the SNP and Yes Scotland: a fear of failure which tied the hands of the pro-independence movement before the starting gun was ever fired.

THE FOURTH ESTATE

"I became a journalist partly so that I wouldn't ever have to rely on the press for my information."

Christopher Hitchens

In post-2014 Scotland, few industries have found themselves as reviled and maligned amongst independence supporters as the Scottish media. From accusations of mere lazy reportage, to perceptions of ingrained bias and a thinly veiled conspiracy to pervert democracy itself, the Scottish media has few friends amongst those who voted Yes in 2014.

In fairness, sections of the media brought this scenario entirely upon themselves; coverage of the referendum was overwhelmingly skewed towards the status quo, and not a single daily newspaper came out in support of the Yes campaign. This would not be such an issue were it not for that fact that it meant the overwhelming mood of the Scottish electorate was patently not reflected in its print press at such a seminal moment in the country's history – but for the notable exception of the *Sunday Herald*.

Did the failure of the Scottish media contribute towards the Yes camp's ultimate defeat on 18 September 2014? Without a doubt. The media onslaught was relentless in its negativity towards the Yes campaign, and at points it was indistinguishable from Better Together's press office communiqués.

Was the failure of the Scottish media to fairly represent both sides in the 2014 campaign a result of bias, though, as is often claimed? Well, obviously, to some degree, there will always be a natural element of bias behind any media outlet, but the extent to which it is or isn't malicious is much less easy to pin down.

To write off the media's entire contribution as mere bias is, *a)* to misunderstand how a newsroom actually works and, *b)* to give far too much credit to the Scottish media.

You see, media hostility towards independence and the Yes movement was entirely predictable. For all the bold claims, the traditional press, as well as broadcast media, are establishment institutions, and as such they rarely cope well with radical challenges to the status quo. This has only become more evident in the years following 2014; you only need to look at the coverage of Jeremy Corbyn's leadership of the Labour Party, or Bernie Sanders' unsuccessful bid for the US presidency. Just as with the 2014 independence referendum, nobody from the commentator class thought either scenario had any traction at the outset, and were bound to react towards them as mere anomalies.

The media in Scotland, like everywhere else, is inherently conservative in its approach to current affairs analysis and adheres doggedly to the *balance fallacy*, which, depressingly, has come to shape the way most of us view political debate.

If you haven't heard of the balance fallacy before, you'll certainly be familiar with its central premise; indeed, it's entirely possible you've been lulled into believing it. It's based around a very simple and somewhat alluring proposition: *that there are two sides to every story, and the truth lies somewhere in between.*

On the face of it, the balance fallacy doesn't really sound like a fallacy at all – in fact it sounds rather intuitive, even fair. It's not, though; it's actually a very lazy – arguably, cowardly – way in which to report controversial stories. Of course, there aren't always two sides to a story: sometimes there's only one, sometimes there are three and sometimes there are a hundred. The assumption that the truth lies somewhere in the middle is an extremely corrosive one, and it's basically an excuse for journalists not to get their hands dirty – or, in other words, not to do their jobs properly.

Adherence to the balance fallacy often results in unequal weighting towards poor political arguments, and the illusion of parity between experts on opposing sides of an argument, but it's most damaging impact is in discouraging broadcasters from covering important stories where they can't find an opposing voice to provide a so-called "balance".

Knowing that the media operates in this way can be a powerful motivator for political campaigns who wish to shut down particular debates. There are occasional, notable instances of "empty chairing", whereby the absence of a speaker is emphasised by a broadcaster – but such examples are the exceptions to the rule.

We could argue the toss about how this affected the coverage of many supposed "battlegrounds" in the 2014 referendum, but it would take us forever – and I'm sure you can think of plenty examples without my help. Where the media's obsession with balance was most damaging to the Yes campaign, though, went largely un-noticed. I'm talking, of course, about the broad grass-roots movement that comprised the vast majority of the campaign.

Probably the most distinctive thing about the media's coverage of the 2014 referendum was the extent to which that wider, non-partisan, pro-independence movement was almost universally ignored. The press and the broad-cast media covered the Yes campaign almost exclusively in terms of Alex Salmond, the SNP, and – to a slightly lesser extent – the official Yes Scotland campaign. This was extremely frustrating for independence supporters, given the huge grass-roots movement that was growing by the day, a non-party movement of genuinely historic proportions which never saw itself reflected in the me-dia.

Many at the time believed this poor coverage was down to unionist bias – indeed many still do. To some extent, of course, there will have been elements of bias, but in reality it had a lot more to do with lazy journalism, and that strict adherence to a supposed balance.

If you're presenting everything as two equally matched campaigns, then by extension you can only cover those things that are represented on both sides. So, the story of an unprecedented, massive, country-wide, peaceful, grass-roots cultural campaign could only have been covered if the opposing No campaign had some-thing similar to balance the coverage out. But it didn't, so it wasn't, and that had the effect of artificially inflat-ing the reach and support of Better Together, as the me-dia always presented it as a unionist mirror image to the independence campaign, which it wasn't.

Perhaps the most transparent example of this was a surreal puff piece by BBC News' Gavin Esler for the As-tro-Turfed "grass-roots" campaign Vote No Borders, set up by millionaire investment banker Malcolm Offord, in association with a PR firm whose previous clients included Israel and the UAE. It was the sort of unquestioning coverage that the many genuine grass-roots campaigns on the Yes side could only have dreamt of. Indeed, the introduction to that package, read by BBC News anchor Anita McVeigh, further illustrated that inability to acknowledge the wider independence campaign:

> "The campaign for Scottish independence appears to be gathering momentum, with the No campaign being criticised by supporters for a lacklustre performance compared to the fiery campaigning of Scotland's First Minister Alex Salmond."
>
> *Anita McVeigh, BBC News (May 2014)*

Or take, for example, the Yes rally in Edinburgh, which took place a year before the vote. The event, which was attended by an estimated 20,000 people, was given equal weighting on the BBC's Reporting Scotland to an entirely staged Better Together leafleting event. The fact that the event was staged is not particularly sinister – most media photo-ops are staged – but the decision to grant it equal significance to a rally attended by 20,000 people ought to raise eyebrows.

For a campaign such as Better Together, the balance fallacy was a godsend. Where there was a huge gap in terms of passion and support between the campaigns, a false impression of parity ensured that those who followed the debate through the media – that being most people – wouldn't realise how disproportionate the coverage was.

Now, many reading this book will be aware that I was involved in the making of *Scotland Yet*. As it stands, it is the only feature film to have been made about the independence referendum, as well as being the first fully crowdfunded film in Scotland. That the Scottish media weren't singing from the rafters about its existence came as little surprise, but the fact that not a single newspaper or traditional media outlet so much as mentioned the film's existence at its time of release – or since – surprised even me. Of the two-hundred-odd who attended the film's premiere at Edinburgh's Cameo cinema, not a single member of the UK press was among them.

This type of media blackout was by no means unique to *Scotland Yet*, of course: much of the Yes movement's activity went entirely unrecorded by the media. In reality, it was practically impossible to get a camera to show up for anything that wasn't a speech by Alex Salmond.

*　　　　*　　　　*

It's generally understood that there was a unionist leaning within BBC Scotland's newsroom, and whilst editorial decisions aren't made en masse, even the most fair-minded observer would struggle to say that the BBC's coverage of the referendum met the standards we've come to expect from our state broadcaster.

We should be careful of assuming there was a conspiracy, however; it's important to remember that newsrooms are, by necessity, dictatorships, and therefore editors' own political leanings are bound to be heavily reflected in the choice and presentation of stories.

A good example of this is the *Daily Record*, an avowedly unionist, Labour Party-supporting paper, many of whose staff were overwhelmingly pro-independence during the run-up to the 2014 referendum, and who were extremely frustrated with the paper's output. But that's just how newsrooms work, and if they didn't operate on such a dictatorial basis, they'd never be able to knock out such a huge amount of copy to such strict deadlines every day. It's an unavoidable trade-off.

Newspapers have always had quite distinctive editorial lines. That's nothing new, and it's not necessarily a bad thing. Indeed, anyone with a subscription to *The National* – arguably the most overtly partisan and biased newspaper in Scotland – would be being pretty hypocritical if they complained that editorial bias in the press was somehow unacceptable.

Broadcasters, on the other hand, are a completely different story; they are bound by specific rules regarding impartiality. As such, accusations of bias against broadcasters such as the BBC are much more serious than those levelled at the press.

One of the major issues faced by Scottish broadcasters is the strange dichotomy inherent in their make-up. On the one hand, they present themselves as a national broadcaster, whilst on the other, their remit is still primarily that of a regional broadcaster – hence the predominance of stories relating to murders and traffic accidents.

When the SNP won its historic landslide in 2011, it was clear that Scottish political journalism was about to play a more significant role than it had previously. Both of Scotland's regional broadcasters, BBC Scotland and STV, had already produced political programming prior to 2011, but the need to step up their game in light of events was glaringly apparent.

STV elected to replace its long-running *Politics Now* programme, which went out on Thursday nights, with the somewhat more substantial, rather glossier *Scotland Tonight*, fronted by John MacKay and Rona Dougall, launching in the autumn of 2011.

The programme was not without its flaws, and its over-reliance on social media content has been the subject of sustained criticism, but overall it was well received and it undoubtedly played a pivotal role in covering the referendum in 2014.

Somewhat ironically, BBC Scotland's politics coverage saw a notable drop in quality as it attempted to address the same problem. *Newsnight Scotland* had been much maligned in its early days – most famously by veteran BBC broadcaster Jeremy Paxman – but over time it had grown in popularity and carved out a niche.

Gordon Brewer had built himself a solid reputation as an informed, fair, yet formidable interrogator, if a tad theatrical at times, and *Newsnight Scotland* certainly held the edge in terms of quality and respectability over STV's *Scotland Tonight.*

For reasons understood by nobody outwith BBC Scotland, a decision was taken to replace the programme with an altogether lighter offering entitled *Scotland 2014.* The new show was a little bit longer than *Newsnight Scotland*, boasted a slightly larger set, and attempted to present itself as more of a magazine programme, covering sport and lifestyle stories as well as politics.

The all-new *Scotland 2014*, fronted by BBC Scotland sports presenter Jonathan Sutherland and former Channel 4 News anchor Sarah Smith, promised to shake up current affairs coverage at Pacific Quay:

> "The opportunity to launch a new programme is not something to turn down anywhere at any time, to front your own show is not something to ever say no to and to be back here covering the most interesting story that's ever happened in Scotland in my lifetime is not something that you could say no to either."

Sarah Smith (2014)[14]

Despite the journalistic prowess of Sarah Smith – and I say that quite genuinely – *Scotland 2014* was a tremendous flop, and never really recovered in the years following the referendum. The programme quickly came to rely on overextended punditry sections drawing on an ever-decreasing carousel of guest commentators, and BBC Scotland ultimately took the decision to axe the programme in 2016, amid embarrassingly low viewing figures.

The damage – or otherwise – to people's understanding of the referendum debate by programmes such as *Scotland Tonight* and *Scotland 2014*, though, is probably not that substantial. After all, these programmes were aimed at a politically literate audience – the sort of people who already knew who Blair McDougall and Blair Jenkins were.

Ultimately, though, the referendum – like any election – was not decided by political anoraks and campaigners; rather, it was decided by those people who don't have the time or the inclination to sit up till half past ten at night watching an obscure debate between Derek Mackay and Jackie Baillie: that is to say, normal people.

These "flagship" shows existed, to a certain extent, in a bubble – the same bubble that all those who were closely engaged in the referendum inhabited. As such, they served as a bit of an echo chamber, often little more than a glossy presentation of the latest Twitterstorm.

The real influence in the broadcast media's coverage of the referendum was in its more mainstream output: its main news bulletins and its radio phone-ins. It is the content of those prime-time programmes which form the foundations of a popular belief that BBC Scotland's newsroom was orchestrating nothing less than a conspiracy against the independence movement. The existence of books like GA Ponsonby's *London Calling: How the BBC Stole the Referendum* is testament to a deep-rooted and widely held mistrust of the Scottish media, but particularly the BBC. Ponsonby's analysis, though, like that of many on the fringes of the independence movement, is misguided. Whilst there was undoubtedly a great deal of one-sided, shoddy reporting emanating from Pacific Quay during the referendum, the assumption that it was a conspiracy to pervert the course of democracy is a big leap.

The bottom line is this: BBC Scotland's flagship news programme *Reporting Scotland* is not the same thing as the *Six O'Clock News*. It may have a similar looking studio, theme tune and graphics, it may appear as part of the *Six O'Clock News*, but it is not the *Six O'Clock News*.

It is true of the media in general, but broadcast media and television in particular holds a certain mystique. To most people it's almost a kind of magic. I've said it before, and I will no doubt say it again: Jackie Bird is just a woman, in a room, reading.

Reporting Scotland is a regional news programme and as such, its staff are not hired on their ability to cover stories of national or international significance – though I'm sure they are more than capable of doing so. Regional news tends to consist of murders, court cases, traffic accidents and sport, with everything else reserved for the main national news.

But that doesn't excuse poor reporting! I hear you cry. No, but it goes a long way to explaining it, and the more we understand about *why* a problem exists, the better placed we are to find a solution. Simply writing off the entire staff of BBC Scotland as establishment stooges will only drive a wedge further between the independence movement and the media, which, if 2014 taught us nothing else, might not be the shrewdest move.

Television news has a lot of influence over how we, as Scots, perceive ourselves, and if we were to see the world from a Scottish perspective every evening, as opposed to a London perspective, the impact on our sense of nationhood would obviously be significant.

Until 2011, BBC Scotland's newsroom was rarely required to cover much in the way of politically significant stories. The sudden step change took everyone by surprise, and the BBC simply weren't equipped to deal with it. Don't get me wrong, there was a great deal of coverage coming from BBC Scotland during the referendum which appeared to be very one-sided, and it did sometimes feel as though they – along with most of the media – were dancing to Better Together's tune. But, as I've already argued in Chapter 2, we were *all* dancing to Better Together's tune, in one way or another.

* * *

The central problem was that time and time again the media, but the BBC in particular, looked as though they hadn't the first idea what they were doing. As 18 September drew closer, it seemed to slowly dawn on the UK's broadcast media that a story of international and historic proportions had been unfolding in their own back yard, and if they weren't careful, Scotland might just go independent before they got there.

This prompted a panic amongst the metropolitan media, who descended on Scotland in a frenzy, with just a couple of weeks to go until the vote. Overnight, we had the surreal situation whereby Scottish journalists, who understood the many twists and turns of the referendum and had been following it since the very beginning, were relegated to the status of mere pundits.

The BBC's former political editor, Nick Robinson, has since pooh-poohed accusations that his understanding of the situation in Scotland was lacking. Indeed, he has suggested that complaints about the BBC's coverage amounted to little more than anti-English racism.

> "There's a deeper question around should a man from London, should an Englishman come to Scotland to cover the referendum, particularly at the last minute? To which my answer is an unequivocal yes ... The idea that before Scotland becomes independent, if she is ever to become independent, that only certain journalists can cover it, who live in certain places and come from certain locations is again dangerous."
>
> *Nick Robinson (2015)[15]*

Ironically, Robinson's words could not have illustrated better his lack of understanding. No one was complaining about where he, or anyone else, was from. There were plenty of London-based journalists who understood the situation in Scotland – often better than those north of the border. Nick Robinson simply wasn't one of them. But why on earth should he have been? His remit was Westminster, not Scotland.

Although the Scottish media coverage of the 2014 referendum was pretty lacklustre, elsewhere in the UK it was non-existent. Indeed, it became a running joke that you were more likely to see Russian, or Iranian TV cameras at a pro-independence rally than UK ones.

I can remember travelling around England prior to the referendum and the vast majority of those with whom I spoke weren't even aware it was happening. More often than not, they would simply stare blankly at me when I brought it up.

Because of that lack of coverage, there was a real void in awareness and comprehension throughout the rest of the UK. As a result, otherwise respectable commentators found themselves relying on facile stereotypes to paper over an extremely shallow understanding of the debate in Scotland, which served to further drive a wedge between the UK media and Scotland's independence movement.

The UK media has historically been regarded as one of the best in the world, and with good reason. So one can't blame people outside of Scotland for assuming it would accurately report what was happening. Now recall that, more often than not, stories about the referendum tended to be accompanied by stock images of people with saltires painted on their faces, a See You Jimmy hat, a still from *Braveheart*, Alex Salmond or a piper. As a direct result of media inertia, these twee nationalistic clichés came to define the debate in its entirety to people outside of Scotland and, in many cases, within Scotland, too.

Essentially, the media – like the SNP back at the start – didn't think there was any traction in the independence debate, and just ignored it. All of this came to a head when crunch time came; the metropolitan media had no real sense of what was going on and had only a matter of days in which to catch up.

As the UK media ran around like headless chickens trying desperately to get their heads around the story, so too its readers looked on bewildered, starved of any contextual understanding or serious analysis, beyond a series of lazy national stereotypes.

Just imagine if all UK election coverage was accompanied with pictures of bowler hats, cups of tea and Morris dancers. With that in mind, spare a thought for everyone living outside of Scotland in 2014.

*   *   *

Without doubt, one of the most influential drivers of

the grass-roots momentum behind the Yes campaign was the extent to which activists and supporters were able to use the Internet to organise and circumvent what many saw as propaganda emanating from our traditional media outlets.

Websites like *Bella Caledonia* and *Wings over Scotland* became valuable resources offering a genuine alternative to the existing media, and the level playing field provided by the likes of Twitter and Facebook allowed ordinary voices, which might previously have gone unnoticed, to question the powerful and argue their case.

From early on, it was clear that the unrestrained, democratic nature of the Web meant that it was difficult to censor ordinary voices or to disguise the size and demographic reach of a grass-roots campaign such as the Yes movement.

The traditional media have always felt threatened by the online world though, and – in fairness – you would too, if you'd had complete control over the flow of information since the invention of the printing press.

It's no coincidence that media coverage of the Internet has, since the early days, been dominated by stories about identity theft, credit card fraud, paedophile rings or online grooming. Quite frankly, they'd rather you stayed away from it entirely and trusted the professionals to keep you in the loop. It's not malicious; it's just self-preservation. It is their livelihood, after all, and there's no question that the Internet poses the biggest threat of all to the entire media industry in its traditional forms.

Politicians, too, are guilty of an ingrained hostility towards the Web – particularly politicians of a more conservative bent. After all, what could be more terrifying than a genuinely free, uncensored, democratic means of communication among the masses?

With the power of the Internet so apparent as the

referendum began to unfold, with ordinary people organising and sharing information online, completely bypassing the media and official campaign literature, something needed to be done – and so the myth of the CyberNat was born …

> "Hunched in front of the flickering computer screen, Brendan Hynes is hard at work, despite the late hour.
>
> The divorced father of three has a look of intense concentration as his fingers race across the keyboard. Like a lot of retirees, the Internet has provided him with a hobby, a useful way of keeping in touch with relatives.
>
> But the former oil industry executive isn't tapping out friendly messages: from his flat in a housing complex in a sleepy Aberdeenshire village, he is spilling endless bile and vitriol onto Twitter, the 'micro-blogging' website.
>
> Hynes has quickly established himself as a 'CyberNat' – the army of online supporters of Scottish independence notorious for their provocative and often abusive comments and now at the centre of a growing political row."

This was the opening gambit to Alan Roden's "exclusive", and somewhat creative, spread in the *Daily Mail* entitled: "CyberNats Unmasked: Meet the foot soldiers of pro-Scottish independence 'army' whose online poison shames the Nationalists" (*Daily Mail*, 25 January 2014)[16].

The article represented the first in a long-running series that would feature in the *Daily Mail* throughout 2014, entitled "CyberNat Watch". The word CyberNat, a pejorative term for independence supporters using social media platforms like Twitter and Facebook, inspired an inexplicably large chunk of hostile media coverage towards the Yes campaign.

Whilst the term itself is generally credited to Labour peer George Foulkes, the subsequent characterisation stems largely from Alan Roden's *Daily Mail* piece.

Roden's portrayal was clumsy but stark; he painted online activists as tragic, lonely figures, who only seem to use the Internet during the early hours of the morning – presumably to insinuate that they're all unemployed losers.

Although the *Daily Mail* spearheaded the CyberNat myth, unionists willingly adopted it as a convenient stick with which to beat their opponents.

It was particularly useful to denigrate online activists, given that this was the very arena in which the Yes campaign was proving most successful. This was territory in which Yes campaigners were not censored at all, and as such they were able to convey their arguments far more successfully than, say, in the pages of the mainstream media.

With the creation of the CyberNat myth, undecided voters could be dissuaded from going online, and discouraged from engaging in the debate – amid warnings that they, too, might suffer the torrents of vile abuse that had supposedly become par for the course amongst online independence supporters.

Of course, there was always the odd nutter who said something offensive, but barely a minute goes by on social media without that happening. It certainly wasn't a phenomenon; rather it was a smear campaign, and a very successful one too.

Most sinister of all was the extent to which online *unionist* abuse actually went entirely unchecked. There wasn't a neat name for it, and it didn't fit into any pre-constructed media narratives, but its presence was overwhelming.

Indeed, the level of online abuse and intimidation from unionists was patently far more ingrained. Its ability to exist without any media acknowledgement or outcry meant that it was less restrained and tended towards a more violent, more sexually explicit tone, including intimidation and even a number of fully-fledged death threats.

There is no question, given the media's preoccupation with so-called CyberNats, that had independence campaigners exhibited such behaviour, it would have been front-page news. As it stands, very few people are even aware that there *was* any intimidation from unionists, let alone the scale of it.

The media can quite legitimately be accused of a number of questionable practices during the 2014 referendum, but that demonisation of online Yes campaigners – whilst completely ignoring their unionist counterparts – was perhaps the most destructive of everything they did.

The perception of online abuse frightened a lot of people away from the debate and stopped them from engaging with the conversation.

Whether said demonisation frightened away that crucial five per cent of the electorate, of course, we might never know.

*　　　　*　　　　*

Polling in the run-up to the 2014 independence referendum was notoriously unreliable, but one thing was consistently apparent: that being the breakdown of votes by age. It's beyond doubt, for example, that older voters were far more likely to favour the status quo. Indeed, it's probably safe to say that the extent to which older voters diverged from the rest of the population may even have swung the entire referendum.

Such a disparity in voting preference amongst older voters is significant, because it correlates pretty neatly with that same section of the population who still consume their news and commentary through the traditional press.

This doesn't prove that the media were biased, of course, but it does strongly suggest that the version of events filtered by the mainstream media must have been significantly different from that which emerged online.

None of this says anything about the voters themselves – each of us is entitled to vote however we wish in a democracy, after all – but clearly the media had an influence on those who consumed it most. Crucially, those for whom the media did have a stronger influence were undoubtedly more inclined to vote No.

In the years since, the media landscape has already seen some big changes, not least the launch of *The National* newspaper.

The National provides comfort to diehard independence supporters, and many – particularly older readers – are grateful to see their politics reflected in a daily newspaper for the first time. In terms of the paper's success in furthering the movement, though, it's less clear.

Newsquest, a company that has never shown any interest in Scottish independence, launched the publication off the back of the referendum. A cynical analysis might surmise that Newsquest simply exploited an opportunity for easy profit from a potential market of 45 per cent of Scots. If profit was their sole aim, that would certainly explain why the newspaper has been so chronically understaffed and under-resourced since its inception. That shoestring budget, alongside its somewhat narrow editorial line, means that *The National* is sometimes more reminiscent of a fanzine than a national newspaper.

One could very convincingly argue that *The National* has, in fact, been somewhat counterproductive for the independence movement. It is certainly now the most overtly biased newspaper in Scotland and, given that its readership was, in days gone by, highly critical of such bias, they now look a little like the proverbial dwellers of glass houses, blithely throwing stones at the walls.

The launch of *The National* also stymied the growth of a genuine alternative media, owned and operated in Scotland. Online efforts such as *Bella Caledonia*, *CommonSpace* and the now-defunct *NewsShaft* struggled to raise even a fraction of the money brought in by *The National*. Indeed, *NewsShaft* was forced to close down entirely as a direct result of chronic underfunding.

Looking ahead to another independence referendum, one wonders just how effective a publication like *The National* would be in aiding a Yes vote. It is not perceived outwith independence supporting circles as providing balanced coverage of Scottish politics, specifically on the constitutional debate. So it's unlikely, in the event of another referendum, that it would be received any differently from those campaign "newspapers" distributed by political parties in the run-up to elections and, in fairness, there are some similarities.

Comforting though it may be in the short term, the solution to bias in the press is not simply to create something that speaks to your own biases. The media should challenge us, and make us question our prejudices, however uncomfortable that might be.

We still have a long way to go. Only when we've nurtured our alternative media to the same extent as we have the likes of *The National* can we truly be proud of Scotland's post-referendum media legacy.

Treating our journalists as though they are little more than unionist stooges, maliciously trying to undermine the hopes and dreams of Scotland, is also a pointless endeavour. It's an attitude which has already created a divide, where many journalists feel disconnected entirely from the independence movement, so great is the animosity they feel.

When the next referendum comes around, the media will still be there, for better or worse. In purely pragmatic terms, the better the relationship all of Scotland has with its media, the better coverage we can expect.

MONEY TALKS

"If you're in trouble, or hurt or need – go to the poor people. They're the only ones that'll help – the only ones."

John Steinbeck

That big business, big money and corporate interests tend to be supportive of the status quo is unsurprising. After all, if you've become wealthy off the back of a particular system, you're unlikely to want to change it.

An uneasy deference to corporate leaders' reverence for the so-called bottom line has become the norm. Whether it's the exploitation of child labour that feeds Coca-Cola's sugar supplies, the actions which brought about the banking crisis or the global arms trade, the ability of big business to prioritise the quest for profit against basic ethics has become humdrum.

Despite an acknowledged ethical gulf, business leaders, particularly obscenely wealthy ones, are routinely held in high regard by governments and the media. There is an assumption that these people are somehow blessed with an insight greater than the rest of us mere mortals, and we have come to see them as bastions of pragmatism and common sense.

Following the now infamous exchange between the BBC's Nick Robinson and Alex Salmond in the week leading up to the 2014 referendum, the Corporation's former political editor received widespread criticism for editing out the First Minister's response to the following question, claiming that "he didn't answer":

> "Why should a Scottish voter believe you, a politician, against men who are responsible for billions of pounds of profits?"
>
> *Nick Robinson (BBC News, Sept 2014)[17]*

It has since been fairly well documented that Mr Salmond did indeed answer the question, namely during the BBC's own live coverage of the press conference in question, but what is much stranger is the extent to which Robinson's premise seemed to go largely unquestioned. So deeply ingrained is our love affair with big business, our fetishisation of captains of industry, that many of us overlooked the far more serious and endemic prejudice at the heart of Nick Robinson's question. As Christopher Silver put it:

> "Journalists are often inclined to take an uncritical view of statements from business leaders, while politicians are viewed as suspect. The logical counter-question, 'why should a voter believe men who are responsible for billions of pounds of profits?' was rarely, if ever, posed to the business community. A failure to interrogate such statements and a tendency to refer to them as objective sources was inherently, if not explicitly, like-

ly to favour a No campaign that was seeking to win by foregrounding the economic risks of independence."

Christopher Silver (Demanding Democracy, 2015)[18]

Whilst business leaders who espoused a pessimistic view of post-independence economics tended to be treated as objective sources, those on the other side of the argument most certainly weren't. Businessmen and women who backed the Yes campaign, for example, tended to be painted as misguided eccentrics with axes to grind.

There are a number of possible explanations for this, some more fanciful than others, but it's hard to ignore many of the more obvious overlaps between the media, big business, and the Better Together campaign.

Perhaps the highest profile example of that crossover came about when the Confederation of British Industry (CBI), which speaks for around 190,000 businesses, declared that it would be officially registering with the electoral commission as a formal backer of a No vote. A CBI spokesperson at the time said:

"The CBI has clearly stated its position in the Scottish referendum debate, that Scotland and the rest of the UK are stronger together as part of the union. We have registered this with the Electoral Commission in accordance with the law."[19]

Shortly after the announcement, a number of high profile CBI members withdrew from the organisation amid complaints that there had been no consultation on the matter. What made this announcement by the CBI so much more controversial, though, was that broadcast media outlets like the BBC, ITV and STV were all members. ITV retained its membership, whilst insisting that it would remain entirely neutral, but STV withdrew, saying:

> "In light of CBI Scotland's decision to register with the Electoral Commission we have no choice but to resign our membership of CBI Scotland forthwith."[20]

The BBC announced that it would temporarily suspend its own membership up to the date of the referendum. However, the Corporation reneged on that, following an embarrassing U-turn by the CBI, wherein they requested that the electoral commission nullify its application.

From the outset, though, it was clear that the Better Together campaign would find its strongest support from within the ranks of big business. Huge sums were donated from the likes of Douglas Flint CBE (Chairman of HSBC) and Ian Taylor (Chief Executive of Vitol Group), who each contributed around half a million pounds.

There was also the largely forgotten Vote No Borders. Officially an entirely separate campaign from Better Together, this "grass-roots, people's campaign" was set up by City Fund Manager Malcolm Offord, alongside consultancy firm Acanchi, whose previous clients included Israel, Bahrain and the UAE.

But it wasn't just money that big business brought to the unionist campaign – though they brought plenty – it was also influence. That influence largely manifested itself in those doom-laden press releases predicting financial collapse that seemed to run on a 24-hour loop throughout the entire referendum.

As proponents of the No campaign were fond of reminding us: *business leaders and employers are entitled to a view on the future of the country*. Quite right, too: everyone is entitled to their view. In fairness, however, the No campaign, alongside the media, often had a tendency to view them as more entitled to that view than the rest of us. But – their disproportionate media reach aside – the opinions of business leaders were obviously just as valid as those of the rest of the population.

What caused a certain degree of understandable uproar was when they attempted to exert undue influence in their capacity as employers. This is exactly what happened to the staff of Barrhead Travel, whose founder distributed an email to 697 of its 800 staff warning them of what he termed "impending disaster":

> "37 per cent of our business comes from England and we would not be able to trade outwith Scotland due to Scotland being outwith the EU and English regulations for at least three years ... The devil is in the detail and as the weeks pass and more is discovered the magnitude of the impending disaster should there be a Yes vote becomes ever more apparent."
>
> *Bill Munro, Director of Barrhead Travel (2014)[21]*

Placing to one side the obvious irony of an argument premised on EU membership, many saw the contents of Munro's email as representing a serious abuse of his position. After all, this was essentially a warning to his staff that they may be out of a job if they didn't vote with their employer.

Widespread criticisms of Bill Munro's email and scores of business leaders such as leisure magnate Duncan Bannatyne, were conveniently dismissed and discredited as – you guessed it: CyberNat abuse.

That thinly veiled threat of job losses as a result of capital flight lay at the heart of the big business case for the Union. For all that our politicians and media idolise multimillionaire business leaders, the general public still tend not to respond well to being told how to vote by rich people, especially where the motivation is to protect their own wealth. With that in mind, it's easy to see why warnings from the likes of BP, RBS, Lloyds Banking Group, Sainsbury's and Asda/Walmart were all framed in terms of Scottish jobs rather than corporate profits.

These sorts of predicted job losses, though, could only ever be premised on one of two scenarios: straightforward vindictiveness, or a lack of demand for those businesses following independence. Since there seems no logical reason as to why newly independent Scots would no longer require petrol, money or groceries, one can only surmise that these were vindictive – albeit empty – threats. Either that, or it was a wilful misinterpretation of what businesses were *actually saying*, as happened with the Edinburgh-based investment company Standard Life.

The narrative that formed around Standard Life's position on the referendum illustrates the extent to which reality could be twisted by the No campaign, whilst simultaneously receiving little or no scrutiny from an acquiescent media.

We all remember what Standard Life had to say with regard to the vote, don't we? Something along the lines of: They'd relocate to England if Scotland voted Yes? "Standard Life could quit Scotland if voters back independence" *(The Guardian)*, "Standard Life to move business south if Scots vote Yes" *(Financial Times)*, "Scottish independence will force Standard Life to move to England" *(Huffington Post)*, "Standard Life boss warns that company will relocate to England if Scots vote Yes" *(Daily Express)*.

As clear cut as this story seemed to be, however, it just wasn't true. The official statement released by Standard Life simply suggested that it would need to register different companies in order to operate throughout the rest of the UK (because it would no longer be the same country). Nowhere in the statement does the organisation so much as hint at relocation following a Yes vote:

> "As a business we have a long-standing policy of strict political neutrality and at no time will we advise people on how they should vote, but we have a duty and a responsibility to understand the implications of independence for our customers and other stakeholders and to take whatever action may be necessary to protect their interests ... In view of the uncertainty that is likely to remain around this issue, there are steps that we can and will take now based on our own analysis. For example, we have started work to establish additional registered companies to operate outside Scotland, into which we could transfer parts of our operations if it was necessary to do so. This is a purely precautionary measure, and customers do not need to take any action. We are simply putting in place a mechanism which, in the event of constitutional change, allows us to provide continuity to customers and to continue serving them, wherever they live in the UK."
>
> *Standard Life Statement (February 2014)*[22]

As the Standard Life "story" broke, a curious thing happened. The above statement was shared in full by independence campaigners online, because – similarly to the Mark Carney situation (see Chapter 2) – it was actually quite a positive story for the Yes campaign.

A very large organisation had essentially said: *Don't worry, whatever happens we're prepared and the sky won't fall in.* But unionist campaigners steered clear of the actual statement entirely, preferring the embellished, heavily edited interpretations churned out by the press.

Unsurprisingly, that fabricated narrative won out, and nowadays few remember what the original statement actually said.

*   *   *

In truth, the influence of big business on the independence referendum existed as part of a larger, more complex problem. Better Together's premise of uncertainty surrounding jobs, pensions and resources allied easily with the big business tendency to favour the status quo. But the killer combination only took effect as it was packaged by a media who, for reasons which still don't make a great deal of sense, seemed entirely unwilling to scrutinise the proclamations of business tycoons.

As a result, the Yes campaign was continually presented as though it was defending itself against reasoned, objective concerns, rather than politically motivated propaganda. On top of that, the ever-cautious SNP and, thus, Yes Scotland – desperate not to alienate the world of business – steered clear of questioning that most corrosive premise: that business leaders' opinions are somehow uniquely objective.

Media attitudes aside, big business always has, and always will, push to influence democratic decisions. We live in a capitalist society, and by definition a capitalist society gives more power and influence to wealthy individuals. Short of changing our entire economic system, there is little we can do to mitigate the influence of big business on future referendums; it will always be one of the most powerful voices in defence of the Union. Powerful though it may be, however, it can't sway entire populations, and history teaches us that it can't hold back the inevitable tide of progress.

THE GHOST AT THE FEAST

*"If you know yourself but not the enemy,
for every victory gained you will also suffer
a defeat. If you know neither the enemy nor
yourself, you will succumb in every battle."*

Sun Tzu

Though independence lost the 2014 referendum, very few would argue that the unionist campaign was victorious per se. Supporters of the status quo prevailed on the day, albeit narrowly, but the general consensus is that they merely won the battle; the war is still very much underway.

The Scottish Conservatives may have emerged unscathed, perhaps even slightly better off, but the real losers of the referendum were the Scottish Labour Party. Utterly decimated at the 2015 General Election, the party, which had dominated Scottish politics for decades, was destroyed and reduced to one solitary MP. Then, in the 2016 Holyrood election under the leadership of Kezia Dugdale, it was relegated to third place in Scotland, behind even the Conservatives.

Victims, perhaps, of their own hubris and an ingrained sense of entitlement, the Scottish Labour Party had been sleepwalking their way towards that moment for the preceding decade; the independence referendum simply fast-tracked their death throes. Labour found itself strung along by a Conservative Party desperate to maintain the dying embers of the Union, yet wise enough to keep well clear of the front lines.

Chewed up and spat out by the Better Together campaign, Scottish Labour found itself isolated and directionless. The party's future is now uncertain, to say the least.

Since time immemorial, Scottish Labour has seemed incapable of, or – perhaps more accurately – unwilling to understand Scotland's independence movement. For decades, the desire for self-determination, alongside the rise of the SNP, was written off as little more than the aspirations of a lunatic fringe. From the Labour Party's perspective, it comprised nothing more substantial than an unhealthy obsession with tartan, bagpipes, Irn-Bru, and dressing up like William Wallace.

The inability to comprehend the independence movement in any terms beyond cornball nationalism was perhaps most apparent during Scottish Labour's 2015 General Election campaign. Few images encapsulate that woeful misunderstanding of the SNP's success quite like that of the then leader of the Scottish Labour Party, Jim Murphy, jogging through Glasgow in a Scotland football shirt, sipping from an Irn-Bru can.

But, independence movement aside, this sort of thing speaks volumes about Labour's understanding of Scotland itself – a nation which can seemingly only be represented via twee nationalistic clichés. Indeed, it implies a deep-rooted contempt for any notion of Scotland as anything beyond a mere electoral region.

That Scotification of Scottish Labour first presented itself during the run-up to the 2007 Holyrood election, when it began to look as though the SNP had a chance of winning. Party political broadcasts were suddenly accompanied by the strains of pipe bands battering out "Highland Cathedral", over clumsily edited footage of saltires and children wearing Scotland football shirts.

The party might have been forgiven for such a shoddy effort back in 2007. That they hadn't made any effort to understand their greatest electoral threat was careless, but that defeat did take them by surprise. That they still hadn't moved on by 2011, or even by 2015, suggests a level of dim-wittedness unrivalled in political history.

The Scottish National Party have, for the last three decades at least, been the greatest threat to Labour's domination of Scotland: a perpetual, living reminder of the party's drift from the left, not to mention its failure to deliver on the promise of a Scottish Assembly back in 1979.

The ranks of the SNP are filled with former Labour members, trade unionists, councillors, even MPs. It is therefore unsurprising that the Labour Party on the whole don't like them and Scottish Labour specifically seem consumed with a hatred towards them.

That loathing of the SNP caused Scottish Labour to see them only through the lens of their own, straw-man caricature of English-hating, blood and soil nationalism. As a result, they remained entirely oblivious to what the SNP actually stood for, or why it wanted independence.

Despite all of that, though, it was the Scottish Labour Party that made all the difference in holding back the tide in 2014; however, in doing so, they lost everything. The party's reputation, its support base, its forty Members of Parliament, even its leader, Jim Murphy: all were sacrificed at the altar of the Union.

Scottish Labour's problem was, of course, born out of complacency. In fairness, that complacency was understandable, and given the sheer dominance the party held over Scottish politics for decades it's little wonder they felt untouchable. Even at the height of that dominance, though, they knew that pressure from opponents – particularly from the SNP – to deliver on a Scottish Parliament was too great to ignore. That isn't to suggest that Scottish Labour didn't play a major role in bringing about devolution, but the legacy of the 1979 referendum, coupled with the devastation of the Thatcher years, reflected poorly on Labour in Scotland and it had left a sour taste.

The Scottish Parliament was up and running within just two years of the 1997 New Labour victory, and whilst it was obviously going to provide a much bigger platform for the Scottish National Party than they'd ever enjoyed, the voting system was engineered in such a way that no party should ever win an outright majority of seats; it wasn't meant to be that kind of parliament.

Despite this brave new voting system, the ranks of Scottish Labour held a certain snootiness towards MSPs who had been elected via the second ballot "list" system. During the first three Parliaments Labour tended to perform well on the first-past-the-post constituency seats, which many in their ranks saw as more legitimate, largely because it mirrored Westminster's voting system.

For that reason, Scottish Labour's front bench team stood only in constituency seats, without the safety net of a place on the list. That decision would come to haunt them in the 2011 election, where the party was all but decapitated in the wake of an SNP landslide.

Not only was Scottish Labour badly defeated, but their front bench was practically wiped out. There were no more potential leaders in waiting – not even any familiar faces. The Labour benches after 2011 were – even by their own standards – second rate, which seriously hampered their ability to provide anything resembling an effective opposition.

It is an open secret that Scottish Labour's MSPs at Holyrood were looked down on by their London colleagues, and treated as second class within the party. It seems ironic now, but to be offered the chance of a seat in the House of Commons was once seen as a promotion, and the "ascension" of the likes of Margaret Curran and Cathy Jamieson saw the establishment – albeit briefly – of a comfortable career path for Scottish Labour politicians.

After the defeat in 2011, Iain Gray's leadership successor, Johann Lamont, took a lot of stick during the 2014 referendum. She wasn't a natural-born leader and she was patently no match for Alex Salmond (but in fairness, few are). Lamont, though, had arguably the toughest job in Scottish politics between 2012 and 2014; her hands were completely tied by her party, and she was forced to defend the indefensible day in, day out. I must confess that I always felt a great deal of sympathy for her.

The thing is, Johann Lamont is clearly someone who got into politics for the right reasons; she's not a careerist and she patently believes in the Labour Party – however misguided one might consider that belief. In taking on the impossible role of party leader during the 2014 referendum, she stepped up when no one else would. It was a thankless task, and I hope her party and her colleagues recognised that.

With all that in mind, the comments she made following her resignation actually seem quite tame:

> "Just as the SNP must embrace that devolution is the settled will of the Scottish people, the Labour Party must recognise that the Scottish party has to be autonomous and not

> just a branch office of a party based in London."
>
> *Johann Lamont (Daily Record, October 2014)[23]*

Despite the opinions of many of her detractors, Johann Lamont is not a career politician, and I suspect the House of Lords has never particularly interested her. However, her lack of presence as a leader throughout the independence referendum was certainly indicative of Scottish Labour as a whole: a party of placeholders, a purposely inferior version of its UK counterpart with no real understanding of what it stood for, beyond woolly protestations about "social justice".

*   *   *

Given the state of the Scottish Labour Party in the years following 2014, it's easy to forget just how strong a position they were in, going into the independence referendum. Considering the SNP's Holyrood landslide of 2011, Scottish Labour's showing at the 2012 council elections was impressive. Whilst they trailed the SNP in second place, the difference in the popular vote was only 1 per cent.

Likewise, the party held on to both their Scottish seats in the 2014 EU Parliamentary election with a 5 per cent increase of the vote share. Meanwhile – at the absolute height of the independence referendum, don't forget – the SNP's share of the vote actually went down, albeit by just 0.1 per cent.

The bottom line is this: during the referendum, Scottish Labour were not the dead duck they in fact became. They looked like a pretty viable option. Pollsters had the

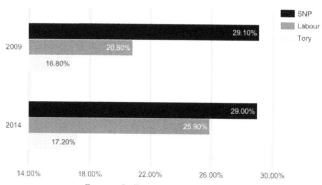

European Parliament Elections, vote share in Scotland 2009/2014

Labour Party leading the Conservatives by a few percentage points for the majority of the last parliament, and there was a real sense that an Ed Miliband government in 2015 was all but a foregone conclusion.

Of course, the pollsters failed miserably to predict the outcome of the 2015 General Election – outwith Scotland at least. But it wasn't just the polls that bolstered that expectation of an imminent victory for the Labour Party at Westminster.

The government representing the unionist vote, and the organisation best placed to fund any campaign to keep the UK together, was the Conservative Party. However much of a brave face that party might put on its ability to appeal to the Scottish electorate, it knew full well the toxicity of the Tory brand north of the Border. The Conservatives, though, valued the retention of the United Kingdom over any sort of Tory face-saving exercise, and that's why Labour's Scottish credentials were talked up so much during that referendum campaign.

The Conservatives might have sounded generous in conceding their inferiority to Labour in Scotland, but that was just political pragmatism. Had the Labour Party seen this for what it was at the time, things may have gone very differently for them. Instead, they allowed themselves to be blindsided by a heady dose of deluded self-importance, cynically exploited by the Tories.

All of this is important as regards the outcome of the independence referendum, because many people were persuaded to vote No in the belief that a Labour government was just around the corner. That subtle, yet powerful narrative permeated the final months of the Better Together campaign, to the extent that many within the Labour Party genuinely came to believe it.

Those of us who took more than a passing interest in politics, however, were under no illusion as to Labour's prospects at the 2015 General Election. Few may have predicted an overall majority for David Cameron's Conservatives, but the prospect of Ed Miliband emerging as Prime Minister was about as likely as Scotland winning the World Cup.

A rose-tinted image of the Labour Party, harking back to the glory days of Clement Attlee's post-war government filtered down through the imaginations of journalists and Labour activists alike. This somewhat creative interpretation of the party couldn't have been credited to any one individual, but a great deal of that work was carried out by former Prime Minister, Gordon Brown, a man who "intervened" in the debate "for the first time" about seven or eight times.

Gordon Brown's contribution to the referendum debate served as a surreal illustration of everything that was wrong with the Labour Party and its stance on Scottish independence. Here was the poster boy for New Labour – the very embodiment of Thatcherite economics – somewhat unconvincingly rejuvenated as a firebrand socialist in the mould of Keir Hardie:

> "We are increasing the powers of that Parliament – faster, safer, better, friendlier change than ever the Nationalists could propose. And proud too that we co-operate and share,

> indeed we Scots led the way in co-operating,
> sharing across the United Kingdom – com-
> mon defence, common currency, common
> and shared rights from the UK pension to the
> UK minimum wage, from each according to
> his ability to contribute, to each according to
> his needs, and that is the best principle that
> can govern the life of our country today."
>
> *Gordon Brown (17th September 2014)[24]*

Brown's speech on the eve of the referendum revealed the extent to which his party had deluded itself as to its own importance. In claiming that "*we* are increasing the powers of [the Scottish] Parliament", he neglected to explain how that could be, given that Labour held power at neither Westminster *nor* Holyrood then – or since.

Labour's sense of its own importance – and complete lack of self-awareness – was probably best illustrated when it sent a delegation of 104 MPs on a train to Glasgow for a photo opportunity on Buchanan Street. Of course, the whole event backfired somewhat, as the show was pretty much stolen by Matt Lygate, a local rickshaw rider, who followed the troops of unamused MPs up Buchanan Street playing *Star Wars'* "The Imperial March" on a loudspeaker, proclaiming: "People of Glasgow! Your imperial masters have arrived!"

Nevertheless, a narrative formed around the Labour Party as being at the core of everything that was British: *sort of* socialist, *sort of* federalist, *sort of* internationalist.

Everything that seemed to be driving the independence campaign – internationalism, a rejection of neo-liberal economics, opposition to nuclear weapons, a hatred of the Tories – should have appealed to those of a traditional Labour mindset. The left wing arguments for the Union were flimsy, to say the least – even George Galloway couldn't make a coherent case for the United Kingdom, no matter how angry he got in the process:

> "Not one person asked in that summer and autumn of 1940 and into 1941 if the pilots who were spinning above us defending us from invasion from the barbaric horde were from Suffolk or Sutherland. We were people together on a small piece of rock with 300 years of common history. That's what they want to break up and all the rest is balderdash."
>
> *George Galloway (June 2014)[25]*

No one thought to "ask" if our World War II allies were from *San Francisco* or *Stalingrad* either, but I don't recall anyone arguing that we ought to have been in a political union with America or the Soviets as a result. But then, perhaps we shouldn't place too much stock in George Galloway's arguments these days. After all, only two years later, he was sharing a stage with UKIP's Nigel Farage, telling us that leaving the European Union would precipitate a socialist utopia in the UK.

So many of the supposedly progressive arguments for the Union – and Galloway's were about as good as they got – lacked any real substance, and it often felt as though many within the Labour Party were all too aware of the flimsiness of their own defence.

By the same token, the Conservative arguments for the Union – whether or not you agreed with them – were completely coherent.

The Tories are unashamedly nationalistic about their Britishness, taking pride and ownership of Britain's colonial past. For the Conservatives, a No vote sought to preserve everything the independence campaign found abhorrent about the British state.

The intrinsically conservative, right-wing argument that essentially defines what the Union represents, would never have washed during the referendum, and even its most ardent cheerleaders were wise enough to see that. So it was with that in mind that Conservatives were able to hand responsibility to the Labour Party to lead the campaign for a No vote. A few appeals to Scottish Labour's inflated sense of importance, and they were putty in the Tories' hands.

The Conservatives pumped plenty of money into the Better Together campaign, but wisely sat quietly in the background, letting their opponents do all the fighting. Because the Tory argument for the Union was as coherent and unchanged as it ever was, the whole experience probably worked in their favour. But Labour's campaign for an utterly contradictory set of nonsensical arguments massively damaged the party's credibility.

Just as the Better Together campaign premised a great deal on the perceived inevitability of a Labour triumph at the 2015 General Election, so too did the Conservative Party. Don't get me wrong, they weren't suggesting it would be their preference, and neither were they making much noise about it, but the Tories were conspicuously quiet about the prospect of a second David Cameron government for the duration of the 2014 independence referendum.

The fear of successive Tory governments that Scotland hadn't voted for was a very real motivator towards independence, and the practical inevitability of that occurring in 2015 was played down to comical proportions. Comical, because Ed Miliband had been a figure of fun since the moment he was "accidentally" elected leader. A less credible PM in waiting we hadn't seen since William Hague in 2001.

Essentially the Labour Party was used. For a short period, the Tories cynically allowed them to indulge in the fantasy that Ed Miliband could win in 2015. By the same token, the UK Party used Scottish Labour, allowing them to indulge in the fantasy that they were still the party of Keir Hardie and the standard bearers of international socialism. Fantasies, all – but that didn't matter: preserving the Union trumped all else.

That willingness to be taken in by the Conservative soft-soaping was fuelled by that infamous sense of entitlement that had come to define Scottish Labour. This, after all, was *their* heartland; independence and the SNP was no more than a risible distraction that would be easily quelled.

Indeed, Scottish Labour was so vehemently opposed to independence that it couldn't even countenance the thought of its party members voting Yes. Organisations such as Labour for Independence were denounced as "SNP fronts", with no high profile Labour figures coming out in favour of a Yes vote, with the exception of Mary Lockhart.

Mary Lockhart was the chair of the Scottish Co-operative Party, which contests elections jointly with the Labour Party. When she announced her intention to vote Yes back in April 2013, she found herself disowned by the party within a week, and was forced to resign. Many saw this as a warning to any other party members considering breaking party ranks. If it was, it was very successful.

It's worth noting that in the intervening years, Mary Lockhart returned to the Labour fold. Indeed, she was responsible for delivering something that Scottish Labour hasn't seen many of since 2014: a local government by-election win against the SNP.

Scottish Labour made much play of her narrow victory against the SNP in The Lochs in summer 2016, claiming that "the tide is turning". The party, however – perhaps characteristically – failed to acknowledge the real significance of that victory, which was that in order to appeal to the left in a post-2014 Scotland, you need a candidate who supports independence.

It's not known how many – if any – Labour MPs or MSPs quietly voted Yes in 2014. I've been assured that some did. Perhaps one day we'll know who they were, but I won't hold my breath just yet.

*   *   *

Scottish Labour's impact on the referendum vote is a bit like that of a bee sting: its effect is somewhat limited.

There's a widely held misconception that bees can only sting once, after which they die. In actuality, bees only die where the victim's skin is thick enough to retain the sting. This, I think, only strengthens the metaphor.

In saving the Union, Scottish Labour laid the groundwork for its own death. Throughout the referendum they were repeatedly warned of this, but they simply couldn't see it. There is no question that the Labour Party was

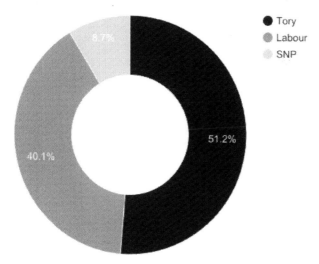

Seat share in the House of Commons,
at the UK General Election 2015

influential during the 2014 referendum; its authority undoubtedly held back a Yes victory. But that was a one-off
trick.

Future referendums over Scottish independence will
not have the luxury of a big-beast unionist party north of
the Border, and neither will they be able to persuade us
that Tory governments are temporary affairs that can be
avoided if Scots would only vote Labour. It is worth re-
membering that whilst Scotland voted overwhelmingly
SNP in the 2015 General Election, it made not a jot of
difference to the make-up of the UK government.

In fact, even if every single Scottish voter had backed
the Labour Party in 2015, nothing would be any different. It's almost as though that's the nub of the matter ...

The post-indyref Yes movement, as well as supporters of the SNP, have taken great pleasure in the downfall
of Scottish Labour, but we ought to be careful not to
overlook the need for credible dissenting voices to fill
that void in Holyrood.

Without that effective opposition, the government
will inevitably suffer. If it isn't kept on its toes, if it isn't
held to account, it will begin to fester. This could potentially present the biggest threat to independence result-
ing from the vacuum left by Scottish Labour, and it is
incumbent on the independence movement to address it.

There is an attitude amongst too many independence
supporters that diversity amongst its party political ranks
is a bad thing, and that a united front entirely comprising
the SNP is the best route towards, *a)* a second referendum and, *b)* independence.

Despite the optimism of much of the movement –
Scotland's independence is unlikely to be won within
anything less than another ten years, and however successful the SNP might be, they will decline in support:
what goes up must come down. The question is this:
When the SNP begins to decline in voter support, where

will those voters turn?

One would like to think that they'd turn to the other pro-independence parties, but since a great many SNP activists have put a great deal of effort into convincing us that those parties aren't to be trusted with the independence cause, it's unlikely.

Don't get me wrong. I'm not suggesting that disillusioned, independence-supporting SNP voters would turn back towards unionist parties, but in lieu of credible alternatives, that only leaves abstention as an option – and apathy has never been the friend of progress.

A return to the days of an apathetic electorate in Scotland would see the SNP stand to lose most, and it would obviously benefit the unionist parties. As support for the SNP dwindled, the lack of any other party supporting independence could easily transport us back to a pre-2014 politics, wherein opponents could decry independence as little more than the partisan obsession of a single issue party with a dwindling support base.

For those who really want to see an independent Scotland sometime soon, the nurturing of an effective, pro-independence opposition is crucial. The pro-union Labour Party is finished in Scotland; now is the time to fill that void.

BETTER TOGETHER AND THE "GREY" VOTE

"Whenever you find yourself on the side of the majority, it is time to pause and reflect."

Mark Twain

In the days following the referendum defeat of September 2014, a correlation became glaringly apparent between voter preference and age, most overtly amongst over-65s and under-25s.

In fact, the No vote among over-65s was actually so great as to potentially skew the result of the entire referendum. If you were to remove those older voters from the equation – though I concede it's a crude measure – the overall result roughly averaged a majority of 54.3 per cent in favour of independence. In fact, amongst every age group except 18–24s and over-55s, the Yes vote triumphed.

As soon as this information began to emerge, however, any attempt to discuss or interpret it was pounced upon by unionists as "attacks" on the elderly, or even as some sort of morbid desire to kill them off in the name of winning a future referendum.

Of course, there were one or two tasteless remarks, but the attention focused on the disparity between older voters and the rest of the population actually had very little to do with the voters themselves. Rather, the data revealed a great deal about the strategy behind Better Together's campaign and the power of what remained of the traditional media.

Better Together has been ridiculed since its inception as a fairly inept organisation; after all, so the observation goes, they managed to turn a solid 15-point lead into just a 5-point lead. In reality though, this was still an impressive feat.

The arguments for independence were – and still are – good, coherent, principled and largely in line with the political outlook of Scotland's electorate, whereas the arguments for the Union have always been pretty ropey. Unless you're an old-school Tory, or a hardened British nationalist harking back to the days of Empire, there aren't really any solid arguments for the Union beyond some economic smoke and mirrors. For that reason, in

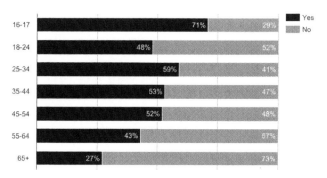

Lord Ashcroft Poll: 2,047 adults who voted in the referendum, by age, interviewed online (831) and by telephone (1,216) on 18 and 19 September 2014[26]

purely strategic terms Better Together's ability to retain the status quo ought to be applauded: in lieu of any solid arguments they still managed to win the vote by 5 per cent. The thing is, during the summer of 2014, it had become slowly apparent that the Better Together campaign was not entirely as it seemed. That is to say, it presented itself as an all-encompassing campaign, aimed at the entirety of Scotland, where in actual fact it had been a lot cleverer than that.

In retrospect, it's obvious that the No campaign effectively wrote off the entire population under the age of 50, concentrating its efforts exclusively on older voters – or, at least, voters with money, pensions and property.

It's a long established truth that as people accrue wealth and assets, so too they tend towards a more individualistic and conservative perspective. Margaret Thatcher knew this and exploited it to great effect by selling off huge swathes of council houses, in the process attracting millions of working-class voters to the Tory party.

> "There is no such thing as society. There are individual men and women, and there are families. And no government can do anything except through people, and people must look to themselves first."

> *Margaret Thatcher (Woman's Own, 1987)*

Just as the Conservatives of the 1980s and, indeed, the New Labour governments of the late 90s and 2000s capitalised on the individualism associated with property ownership, so too did Better Together.

In contrast, the Yes campaign was all about society and the coming together of the entire population for the common good.

Yes was, without doubt, the more successful campaign in that it had all of the momentum, and it was the only campaign to consistently increase its support throughout the run-up to 18 September 2014. Regardless of that, however, the Yes campaign still lost, essentially because of Better Together's strategy of appealing to individualism and conservatism.

So why would that perspective be most prevalent amongst older voters? Well, it's not that older people are more selfish, far from it; but logically they are more likely to own property or to have accumulated assets over the course of their lifetime. As a demographic they tend to have the most to lose materially, hence so much of the unionist message was centred on the notion of financial uncertainty.

It is actually a testament to Better Together's strategic prowess, given how shambolic and out of touch they appeared throughout the entire process, that they successfully targeted their message and resources to maximum effect. They were fighting an uphill battle from the get-go, so to emerge with a 5 per cent lead is far more impressive than they are ever given credit for.

That sort of hard-headed, cynical strategy is something which Yes Scotland could have done with, but as we already know, there was no effective strategy to win the referendum at Yes Scotland, largely due to the overbearing influence of the SNP, who lacked faith in the campaign from the outset.

Better Together was widely derided for its overwhelming emphasis on negativity, especially when the internal codename "Project Fear" leaked out, but in reality, uncertainty was their only trump card.

As we'll discuss in Chapter 8, fear is one of the greatest motivators we have as human beings: we have fear to thank for our survival as a species. But fears can be manipulated and exploited, and the campaign to maintain the United Kingdom did that with a relentless zeal.

The Better Together campaign made great play over questions, for example, regarding the safety of pensions in the event of a Yes vote, which, combined with a ramped up sense of uncertainty over currency, presented a genuinely frightening prospect for many Scots.

Unnerving though these questions may have been, the No campaign went out of its way to ensure that any information that might put minds at ease was brushed under the carpet. For example, Better Together did not – for obvious reasons – acknowledge the statement from the UK Pensions Minister guaranteeing continuity. Obviously, a No vote was of far greater value than peace of mind for Scottish pensioners.

*   *   *

Of the many explanations as to why over-65s voted so differently from every other age group, the most likely regards access to information. After all, whilst it's true that older voters tend to be a bit more conservative, and opinion polling does support that notion, one major factor that separates older voters from the rest of the electorate is that, by and large, they tend not to use the Internet.

An ONS survey[27] from 2015 showed Internet usage amongst 16–54 year-olds at well above 95 per cent, dipping slightly to 87 per cent for 55–64 year-olds; but the figure drops off dramatically to 71 per cent at age 65, and just 33 per cent for over-75s. Moreover, according to research carried out in 2015 by *Ofcom*[28], those over-65s who are online are much less likely to use it as a source of information.

But how does any of this relate to the independence referendum? Well, it's probably fair to say that the Internet was the single biggest factor in building and nurturing the massive grass-roots campaign for a Yes vote. The Internet gave voice to thousands of individuals. It allowed stories to be shared, discussed and often debunked at the click of a mouse button. The Yes campaign grew into a Scotland-wide community of ordinary voters, and social media sites like Facebook and Twitter acted as a unifying force, hugely facilitating its strength in numbers.

It wasn't just social media that breathed life into the Yes campaign, though. So, too, did the flourishing alternatives to the traditional press. From highfalutin think pieces, snarky analysis, political satire and podcasts to television talk shows, the Internet was way ahead of the mainstream press in terms of energising the debate.

The Web served as a democratising force that gave a voice to a campaign that would have otherwise been frozen out by a hostile media.

For Better Together, the Internet presented a major threat, as it made it utterly impossible to control the flow of information. In light of that, it makes a great deal of sense that the campaign would closely concentrate its efforts on that specific demographic who wouldn't be reached by social media.

As for the rest of the population, they were simply encouraged not to engage with the online debate for fear they might fall victim to "abusive attacks" from so-called CyberNats. It's really all quite transparent when you look at it in context.

Older voters are more likely to buy a daily newspaper too, and, famously, not a single Scottish daily endorsed a Yes vote. Indeed, the newspapers tended to follow a rather boring version of the referendum as set out by Better Together press releases. In fairness, that narrative was authenticated substantially by a shambolic Yes Scotland, which was only too happy to provide daily,

SNP-sanctioned sound bites about currency unions and the like.

For those who argue that Scotland's media was overwhelmingly biased against independence, the skewed preference of older voters in the 2014 referendum certainly aids their case. That said, it doesn't necessarily prove anything with regards bias, nor does it prove that older voters were somehow denied accurate information – but it does support the notion that they were consuming *different* information.

Better Together wasn't just about information though. To a large extent it was about encouraging people not to engage with the debate. Unionists were effectively urged to sit tight and refrain from talking to anybody about it.

Representatives of Better Together, alongside many No voters, proudly referred to themselves as belonging to "the silent majority" during the latter days of the referendum. This is a distinctly sinister type of politics, which actively commends people for rejecting debate or critical thinking.

The term "silent majority" has historically referenced – indeed applauded – conservative electorates who avoid public discourse and debate, the phrase being popularised by US presidents like Calvin Coolidge, Richard Nixon and Ronald Reagan. Donald Trump's 2016 Presidential campaign is probably the most contemporary usage. So Better Together's don't-get-involved strategy is in excellent company – if, that is, hard right conservatism's your thing.

It speaks volumes about a campaign when one of its core messages is to encourage its supporters to avoid and even fear debate. *If you're planning to vote No, just keep quiet and sit tight.*

This was more than just an aversion to debate, though. The wider Yes campaign was an exciting, hopeful, diverse and inclusive movement, which contrasted starkly with the somewhat grey, corporate No campaign, and redressing that imbalance made up a large chunk of the Better Together narrative. A palpable effort was made to paint the largest grass-roots campaign in Scottish history as a "loud minority", whose enthusiasm represented nothing less than a sinister and calculated campaign to "shout down" its opponents.

> "[Unionists] don't expect to be shouted down or to be fearful if they speak out. Now that's not the sort of Scotland I think any of us want to live in. We want to live in a country where there is freedom to say what you think you believe in."

Alistair Darling (GMTV, September 2014)

In fact, wherever large numbers of independence supporters assembled, opponents were quick to paint them as intimidatory. This phenomenon was perhaps best illustrated by Labour's so-called street fighting man Jim Murphy, who seemed to think it unacceptable that ordinary people might have the audacity to turn up and heckle an MP in a public square. Surely, this is the very essence of democracy?

> "The Yes Scotland campaign has organised mobs to turn up at every meeting that I'm taking part in to try and silence undecided voters and to try and intimidate me."

Jim Murphy (August 2014)[29]

Far from the "organised mobs" of Jim Murphy's fevered imagination, this was a flashpoint in Scotland's democratic history. After all, how often do voters get the chance to challenge their elected representatives in a public space? It was in many ways a beautiful thing.

For all the talk of violence and intimidation which supposedly emanated from the Yes campaign, it was a fiction. But it was a fiction with a strategic purpose, and it brought with it some sinister side effects. In ramping up the idea that Yes campaigners were intolerant and violent, it actually caused such ill feeling as to bring about an unnerving number of *genuine* violent incidents perpetrated by unionists. Somewhat ironically, it was these incidents that accounted for almost all of the – thankfully rare – referendum-related violence.

> "As the polls turn against them, Unionists and the media continue to irresponsibly incite anger among groups of people with a track record of nationalist violence [...] Only one side will win if the No camp is allowed to turn the most peaceful independence campaign in world history into a civil war."
>
> *Stuart Campbell, Wings Over Scotland (April 2014)[30]*

Despite the peaceful nature of the Yes campaign, an impression was cultivated by its detractors of an aggressive, intolerant, even violent, mob. By stark contrast, any violence from the unionist side was largely ignored: incidents ranging from chairs thrown at canvassers from balconies, an assault on an OAP and numerous death threats against Alex Salmond, to the mass unionist riots in Glasgow's George Square on 19 September 2014.

Ultimately, the campaign to save the Union was really focused on two objectives: targeting its message at the most conservative and least Web-savvy sections of the Scottish electorate, and discouraging voters from engaging with the debate by stoking up notions of an aggressive, intimidatory Yes campaign.

That strategy of focusing resources, combined with a relentless smear campaign against pro-independence activists was, of course, successful. That said, a lot of that success stemmed from the Yes campaign's inability to see what Better Together was actually up to. Ironically, it was so preoccupied with the job of combatting a relentless smear campaign, that it completely missed the main attack.

*   *   *

Despite ever-dwindling readerships, the referendum demonstrated that the value of the traditional press is more than just financial. The media's influence over the outcome of the 2014 vote was undeniable, and that influence undoubtedly favoured the Better Together campaign.

In many ways, though, online journalism presented a common enemy between the unionist campaign and the mainstream media, as both institutions were ultimately less influential as a result of the democratising power of the Internet. It's no coincidence that politicians are forever trying to regulate and control online activity, whilst the media paints the Web as little more than a terrifying hotbed of abuse, fraud, identity theft and paedophile rings.

The Internet is still in its infancy, and who knows what it will have evolved into by the time of another referendum? With each passing day, however, the playing field is levelling. As websites like *Wings Over Scotland* now compete with major newspapers in terms of readership figures, what constitutes journalism and how we consume it continues to change at breakneck speed.

The 2014 independence referendum was in effect the last throw of the dice for the Scottish media – one last chance to flex its ageing muscles. It is odd to think, of course, and it is somewhat ironic, that the industry's future might have been a great deal more promising in the wake of a Yes vote.

With regard to Scotland's elderly voters, who found themselves so massively out of step with the rest of the electorate, the Yes campaign must understand that it failed to reach them.

Yet again, potentially millions of votes were lost due to a lack of strategy from Yes Scotland and the SNP – and even if they had managed to understand what Better Together was doing, their inability to translate it to the activists on the ground, in lieu of any coherent strategy, would have rendered it entirely useless information.

THE FORCES OF NATIONALISM

"He is no lover of his country, that unnecessarily disturbs its peace. Few errors and few faults of government, can justify an appeal to the rabble; who ought not to judge of what they cannot understand, and whose opinions are not propagated by reason, but caught by contagion."

Samuel Johnson

One of the most misinterpreted quotes of all time is Samuel Johnson's "patriotism is the last refuge of a scoundrel". It's a phrase that's become shorthand for the idea that nationalism is almost always a cover for something malevolent or self-serving. In fact, Johnson was expressing the very opposite sentiment: he was extolling the virtues of patriotism and love of one's country through an embracing of the status quo.

In many ways, that cultural view of nationalism and patriotism still holds true. That is to say, *provided you are on the side of the governing elite, patriotism is a be-*

nevolent force.

In terms of Scotland's independence movement, nationalism or patriotism per se have never really played significant roles. Of course, this is practically impossible for a lot of people to get their heads around, because so much of the narrative against independence has centred on an imagined hotbed of parochial nationalistic sentiment. But, as with all successful narratives, its power isn't drawn from tangible evidence – rather, it's the inevitable result of having been repeated so often.

By ironic contrast, there has been a noticeable increase in British nationalism over the last decade; long before Brexit, there was Gordon Brown's campaign for an allotted day in which to celebrate British identity and even "honour" the Union flag, to the state propagandists' wet dream of the London 2012 Olympic Games' opening ceremony.

British nationalism is something that is embraced by the UK government and our media as a benevolent representation of all it means to be British. Whether that's Wills and Kate, Sam Cam on the *Bake Off,* or a cup of tea emblazoned with the words "Keep Calm and Carry On" British nationalism is something we're encouraged to take pride in. Scottish nationalism is not. Scottish nationalism, according to its detractors, is a dangerous and malevolent force.

The 2014 independence referendum had a very strange relationship with nationalism. British nationalism became hugely amplified, but it was rarely acknowledged for what it was. Yet, simultaneously, the Yes campaign was presented at every turn as a malign, narrowly nationalistic movement, which it most definitely wasn't.

> "This is how war starts: a charismatic leader convinces a group of people that their economic hardship is caused by another group which dominates state institutions. The an-

swer is to bring down those institutions and drive the 'other' group out. Neighbours are pit against one another. Conflict erupts into violence."

Lucy Turner, Independent (September 2014)[31]

In many respects, the Better Together campaign positioned itself as an antidote to an entirely imagined nationalism – a nationalism that sneakily and cleverly hid its xenophobic sentiment behind a carefully maintained veil of progressive internationalism.

Better Together responded to that fictitious independence movement by proclaiming its love for all things Scottish, namely tartan, bagpipes, shortbread and Tunnock's Tea Cakes, whilst emphasising, for good measure, that they didn't hate the English.

The accusation that the independence movement was motivated by an underlying Anglophobic sentiment was one of the more poisonous elements of the No campaign's armoury. I mean, all's fair in love and war, but that sort of thing's not really cricket.

In reality, huge swathes of the Yes campaign was – and continues to be – made up of English people and – as Better Together were fond of pointing out – there's hardly a soul in Scotland who doesn't have family or friends south of Gretna.

The accusations of Anglophobia were, to most people, an obvious and transparent smear, designed to keep people distracted from the genuine arguments for independence. Arguments centred first and foremost on a political campaign. It was about representation. It was about a rejection of the politics of neoliberalism and repairing an archaic democratic deficit inherent in the deeply unfair Westminster system.

The campaign which harnessed nationalistic sentiment most during 2014 was the No campaign, its spokespeople feeling compelled to emphasise their "Scottishness" at every turn. Perhaps the most cringe-worthy example of this was *Torchwood* actor John Barrowman's video appeal for Better Together, in which he donned a tartan jacket and actually *put on* a cod Scottish accent to angrily defend his right to an opinion on the referendum – something that no one, at any point, had attempted to deny him.

> "Like hundreds of thousands of other proud Scots, my work means that I have made my home in another part of the UK, this means that I won't have a vote in September. However, I am Scottish, I do have an opinion, and I do have a voice."

John Barrowman (January 2014)[32]

Mysteriously, very little was done by the media to dispel that impression of an ingrained Anglophobia. The campaign group English Scots for Yes, for example, got virtually no coverage; likewise the backing for Yes amongst high profile English activists like George Monbiot, Ken Loach, Tariq Ali and Billy Bragg went pretty much unreported.

Despite the multitude of high profile Better Together activists perpetuating the bogeyman of anti-Englishness, it is heartening to note that the narrative never fully took hold among the electorate. After all, it's hard to maintain an accusation of such magnitude without a single tangible example. That in itself must have been extremely frustrating. As the commentator Stephen Daisley once quipped: "some unionists will never forgive the SNP for not being the party they desperately want it to be"[33].

In fairness to a lot of unionist campaigners, many refused to be lured by the Anglophobia smear. Prominent

Better Together activist, Constitutional Lawyer and subsequently Conservative Party MSP Adam Tomkins, for example, had little time for the idea that Anglophobia played any significant role in the Yes campaign:

> "I don't really particularly identify myself as English any more, but a lot of people here would identify me as English. I have a reasonably high profile in the [Better Together] campaign, and I have never had any anti-English abuse. I don't think I've ever been discriminated against in Scottish public life because I didn't come from Scotland, but moved here. No, I don't feel that the way in which the campaign has been conducted is really fuelled by anti-Englishness."
>
> *Professor Adam Tomkins (2014)[3]*

Nevertheless, a fear of Anglophobic reprisals following a Yes vote still existed, and will have undoubtedly led a number of English-born voters to have been nervous about independence, especially when those fears were being stoked by various high-profile unionist tub-thumpers via the pages of a sympathetic press:

> "Many 'No' campaigners accuse Alex Salmond of quietly stoking [anti English] tensions. Both [George] Foulkes and Jill Stephenson, an emeritus professor of history at Edinburgh University, believe the SNP leader and his colleagues often speak in anti-English 'code'... 'Any time you hear senior members of the SNP complain about "Westminster", or "the Tories", or "London", what they are really talking about is the English. And supporters know it,' says Stephenson."
>
> *Daily Mail (September 2014)[34]*

To independence supporters, the idea that anyone truly believes that words like "Westminster", "Tories" or "London" represent some sort of secret code for English people is both tragic and laughable, not least because the English population suffers just as much at the hands of the UK's London-centric political system as Scotland does.

Despite all of this, many unionists genuinely believed that the Yes campaign was little more than a manifestation of a deep-seated hatred for our English neighbours, and newspapers like the *Daily Mail* did all they could to inflame those fears.

It's worth pointing out, of course, that there is an element of Anglophobia in Scotland, but it's no greater a phenomenon than any other type of racism, and it's certainly not confined to one particular viewpoint on the constitution.

Perhaps the most glaring contradiction with regards nationalism and the referendum, though, is the extent to which British nationalism was overlooked. In terms of xenophobic – even fascistic – leanings, the No campaign played host to a smorgasbord of intolerance and insular politics. It is telling that *every single* far-right political organisation in the UK backed the Better Together campaign – UKIP, The Orange Order, the BNP, Britain First, the SDL. Whilst those groups obviously didn't make up a majority of No voters, it is worthy of note, in the context of a discussion about nationalism and xenophobia, that they so universally opposed the Yes campaign.

But then, of course, the far-right had no truck with the independence movement as it represented in so many respects a rejection of old-fashioned ethnic nationalism. The Yes campaign of 2014 was arguably the most open, progressive, internationalist movement that Scotland has ever seen. After all, it would be a very strange brand of insular nationalism that argued for looser immigration controls and greater integration with our European and

Scandinavian neighbours.

One of the most impressive feats of Scottish union-ism is the extent to which its narrative is so glaringly at odds with reality. Essentially, British nationalism has al-ways been a deeply conservative concept, idealising the image of a nation forged off the back of colonialism and empire, prioritising class and status over modern ideals of democracy. By contrast, Scottish nationalism has al-ways been, by and large, a movement of the left, and despite what many of its detractors might like to believe, the Scottish National Party has, since its inception, em-braced an internationalist, civic nationalism.

Accusations of Anglophobia against independence campaigners are nothing new; it's an old slur. This quote from the first-ever socialist member of the UK parlia-ment, a founding member of the Scottish Labour Party and ultimately first president of the Scottish National Party, illustrates the reality rather well:

> "The enemies of Scottish nationalism are not the English, for they were ever a great and generous folk, quick to respond when justice calls. Our real enemies are among us, born without imagination."
>
> *RB Cunninghame Graham (1934)*

For all the strange dichotomy between Scottish and British nationalism seems unfair, however, not to men-tion a tad hypocritical, it's just the way the world works.

Established nation states will always enjoy the luxury of nationalism as a positive thing – indeed, a cultural right. It's far too useful a tool for any government not to utilise, after all. Whether it's the Queen's Jubilee, the Fourth of July or a military parade in Pyongyang, the reinforcement of a shared national identity is powerful.

For exactly the same reasons, similar displays of nationalism from mere aspiring nation states will always be branded as parochial and malevolently xenophobic. It almost goes without saying that any display of nationalism which undermines that of the ruling government would be frowned upon or ridiculed by those who wish to retain the status quo.

Until such nations achieve independence from the dominant state, all displays of national unity risk falling victim to misrepresentation and smears.

That goes a long way to explaining why unionists are able to overlook the fascistic elements within their support base: *their* nationalism is accepted as an ordinary, essentially benign force.

So, somewhat depressingly, there's little point in crying foul over the obvious contradictory attitudes towards British and Scottish nationalisms.

That Scottish nationalism is overwhelmingly civic and internationalist is irrelevant to its detractors. Only following independence will Scotland's sense of self be treated equally to that of any other nation's – benign or otherwise.

THE FEAR FACTOR

"It is not power that corrupts but fear. Fear of losing power corrupts those who wield it and fear of the scourge of power corrupts those who are subject to it."

Aung San Suu Kyi

Fear is arguably the most powerful motivator at our disposal; indeed, it has served as one of the cornerstones of humanity's evolution. Whether we're running away from sabre-toothed tigers, steering clear of lightning bolts or attempting to clear a minefield, natural selection has always been reliant on fear as a valuable and often life-saving emotional response.

Study after study has shown that our decisions are overwhelmingly influenced by fear – particularly fear of the unknown, and most analysis of the 2014 referendum result would suggest that fear played a major role in the eventual result.

Better Together is now widely acknowledged to have been a campaign premised on fear; indeed, the term "project fear" was embarrassingly revealed as one of its internal code-names during 2014. It should be noted that the campaign's communications director, Rob Shorthouse, has subsequently claimed that the term was a joke – merely a response to incessant accusations of scaremongering; but campaign chief Blair McDougall later conceded that despite sustained criticism, negativity was a key plank of the campaign:

> "If you do your own research and you get really clear messages back from it, have the courage to stick to it regardless of what the commentators are saying. Because they have an increasingly small reach in terms of setting the agenda."

> *Blair McDougall (September 2014)[35]*

The Scottish electorate was famously encouraged to be very afraid over the course of the referendum campaign, whether that was at the mere prospect of financial meltdown or at the possibility of an all-out North Korean-style dictatorship with a deified Alex Salmond at its helm. But few No campaigners overstated the dangers of independence to quite the extent that former foreign secretary George Robertson did:

> "For the second military power in the West to shatter this year would be cataclysmic in geopolitical terms … Nobody should underestimate the effect all of that would have on existing global balances, and the forces of darkness would simply love it."

> *George Robertson (April 2014)[36]*

Worry not, I'm not going to bore you by debunking all

of Better Together's many scare stories – that has been done pretty comprehensively already – but it's important to acknowledge the common thread that ran through the innumerable scares rustled up by the No campaign. That is to say, they were, without exception, hypothetical scenarios, which by definition were impossible to prove or disprove.

For example, there was never any solid evidence that a currency union wouldn't have prevailed. Likewise, the EU expressed no position either way regarding Scotland's status post-independence (placing to one side the increased consensus on continued membership post-Brexit); and despite billboards and videos to the contrary, fears about pensions and mass unemployment were founded on no tangible evidence. But it was their hypothetical unprovability that made those scare stories so effective, appealing, as they did, to our natural, instinctive desire to be safe rather than sorry.

In the final months of the referendum, Better Together released a TV ad campaign entitled "The woman who made up her mind", which posited that the issues were essentially too complex for most ordinary people to get their heads around, and that the arguments against independence were simply too plentiful to ignore. The advert featured a supposedly busy mother, played by an actress, complaining about the extent to which people – specifically members of her own family – were taking an interest in the referendum:

> "There's not much time left for me to make a decision, but there's only so many hours in the day, and there's a lot to weigh up. I mean – could we keep the pound? The guy off the telly promises us we can – 'it'll all be fine' he says. Yeah right, I've heard that one before."
>
> *Better Together: The woman who made up her mind / Saatchi & Saatchi (2014)*

The advert was widely ridiculed by independence supporters for its patronising overtones as well as its overt promotion of apathy and contempt for political debate. That said, the video tested extremely well with undecided voters and, fundamentally, it did represent the attitudes of huge swathes of No voters – people who were largely disengaged from the campaigns and whose knowledge of the referendum was defined, for the most part, by the narrow and overwhelmingly negative picture painted by the media. It's no wonder they were terrified.

Of course, Better Together's more active supporters would probably reject the assertion that they were frightened, favouring terms like "cautious" or "prudent", but given that their warnings were based entirely on hypothetical scenarios in an imagined future, they could only really have been defined as fears. Besides, it tends only to be in the face of fear that one exercises caution or prudence.

Since 2014, a number of people have expressed incredulity that a campaign so negative as Better Together could have defeated a positive one such as that run by Yes Scotland. The truth is, however, that a campaign based on fear was always bound to be victorious. The really impressive feat was that given that context, Yes did as well as it did.

*   *   *

We humans like to think of ourselves as extremely rational, but a great deal of psychological research tends to point to the complete opposite: we are in fact pretty irrational, illogical and superstitious by nature. Even where the outcomes of our decisions appear entirely unambiguous or self-evident, emotion plays a key role.

The Yes campaign prospered because so many people were able to place their natural emotional responses – namely fear of the unknown – to one side, in favour of the arguments. The No campaign prospered in exactly the opposite way, by encouraging people to embrace their most base emotional response to the prospect of change, and to fear the arguments.

None of this is to imply that No voters were stupid, or somehow unwitting victims of elaborate mind games – rather, that they were human. Since time immemorial, fear of change has propped up the status quo. Nonetheless, that's not to say that psychological tricks weren't employed to shape the way voters reacted to the proposition of independence.

From early on in the campaign, it became clear that both sides had adopted very different vocabularies in describing the consequences of a Yes vote: Yes Scotland spoke in terms of "independence" or "self-determination", where Better Together tended to go for terms like "separation" or "breaking away". This is not insignificant, and a number of classic psychology studies suggest that the more dramatic, negatively charged language of the No campaign would be more effective and influential in shaping the way in which people processed the arguments.

It's not simply a question of effectively transmitting the arguments, though; many of us are simply incapable of understanding, or believing, information which contradicts that which we already believe. We all like to think we're open-minded and that our opponents are not, but in truth, each of us brings a certain amount of bias – or, as psychologists would put it, confirmation bias – to the table.

Confirmation bias refers to the natural human tendency to look for, interpret, favour, and better remember information which allies with our existing beliefs. We all do it, and, perhaps unsurprisingly, it tends to be more prevalent when we are dealing with political or emotionally charged issues.

In short, even when the facts are readily available, if they contradict our existing beliefs we are all fully capable of rejecting them on principle without even being aware that we're doing it.

That inherent bias towards one's own world view is obviously not unique to No voters, but it will have helped the No camp far more than it did the Yes camp. The two campaigns had very different jobs in the run-up to the referendum: Yes had to persuade around 20 per cent of Scots to change their minds, whereas No simply had to ensure they didn't. Clearly, then, an instinctive rejection of new information – no matter how accurate – which contradicts your own beliefs, would have been extremely useful to the campaign that started the process ahead in the polls.

The most depressing take-home message for the Yes campaign, though, is that even if it could somehow have proven the case for independence *beyond any reasonable doubt*, that still wouldn't have guaranteed changing a single voter's mind.

*　　　*　　　*

From the very beginnings of the 2014 independence referendum, the decision was presented as a perpetual tug of war between the head and the heart: would we vote based on an emotional reaction to the question, or a logical, hard-headed one?

Whilst it's true that the decision was divided between emotion and logic, it's not the way round that most of us have come to think of it. The orthodox view suggests that Yes voters were misty-eyed romantics caught up in a rose-tinted view of Scotland, whilst No voters, though no less fond of Scotland, were more economically literate, hard-headed pragmatists. Therefore, conventional wisdom has it that the head won out over the heart. But that's just another narrative peddled by a victorious unionist camp to retrospectively undermine the credibility of the independence movement.

On 18 September 2014, *the heart won out over the head.* By this, I mean that emotion won out over logic. In the end, it was fear that swayed the vote, fear of the unknown and a fear of change. But, to reiterate, fear is a perfectly natural human response. Study after study shows just how hardwired we are to resist change; even where we can be convinced with absolute certainty that change will make us better off, we're often more likely to stick with what we know. Most of us have stayed in horrible jobs longer than we probably should have, or kept going with a failed relationship well past its sell-by date; fear of change is a powerful motivator, and we're all guilty of it.

Many unionists would chuckle at the notion of the Yes campaign as a logical, informed movement; but then, they did spend three years being told that Yes was made up entirely of economically illiterate, sentimental xenophobes.

Frustratingly, the media had a tendency to present the argument as a fairly two-dimensional one about currency, "economic uncertainty", oil or even Anglophobia. This was somewhat exasperating for the independence movement, which almost never saw itself – or indeed its arguments – reflected accurately.

Yes 2014 was a multicultural movement, which cared not a jot about North Sea oil, ancient Scottish history or even the SNP. It was a movement which saw swathes of ordinary Scots reading about, and discussing, issues like land reform, Scandinavian tax models, housing, renewable energy, culture and alternative media; a movement which was thinking long and hard about the sort of future Scotland it wanted to inhabit. Yet all too often it was portrayed as little more than a partisan personality cult inspired by a few too many viewings of *Braveheart*, with Alex Salmond occupying the role of Scotland's very own Pied Piper of Hamelin.

Contrary to popular belief, Yes voters weren't taking some kind of blind punt. In fact, one of the defining features of the 2014 independence movement was its thirst for information, because ultimately the desire for independence was premised on what it would allow Scotland to do next. It makes sense that the battle cry of most town hall meetings during the campaign was: *The real work begins on the morning of 19 September.*

Admittedly, No voters could be forgiven for missing this mass flourishing of civic engagement, largely due to unwillingness in the media to acknowledge its existence.

The informed, methodical, thought-out "head" vote was exemplified by the Yes campaign. These were the people who had devoted an unparalleled amount of their time to researching and understanding that potential future Scotland which only independence would make possible.

I should stress that I'm not saying all unionists were poorly informed, or that they took no interest in Scotland's future; many did – it's just that, by definition, they didn't see independence as an opportunity for positive change. In that scenario, it's perfectly understandable that spending hours of free time reading up on all the significant things Scotland could achieve in the event of a Yes vote would hold little appeal.

That said, whilst it's true that many No voters gave a great deal of thought to the idea of independence, it's also true to say that the Better Together campaign was one which relied on – indeed, encouraged – apathy and disengagement. That was perhaps illustrated most starkly in Gordon Brown's eve of referendum speech, during which he encouraged those who felt they didn't know enough about the proposition to *vote against it.*

> "If you have any doubts … if you are thinking of the future of Scotland and if you don't know, the answer has to be no."
>
> *Gordon Brown (17 September 2014)[23]*

Compare that to the independence movement's war cry to get informed, to read more, to speak to people, to ask questions, and it's clear to see how much Better Together relied on people's fear of the unknown. Sure, it was a dirty tactic, but it ultimately won the day.

The independence movement should be careful not to buy into the notion that its campaign was premised on emotion, because it wasn't. By the same token, the unionist campaign should never be allowed to get away with claiming it was guided by the head, because it wasn't. The No vote was guided by an emotional gut response to the fear of change – no specific change, just change in general. This may be one of the most important myths that we dispel in the wake of 2014's defeat.

With all that in mind, we'd do well not to get sucked in to the idea that the Yes campaign's arguments weren't somehow strong enough. As masses of psychological research shows, most people can resist even a sure thing if it involves any kind of major change.

The independence campaign does not need to become more hard-headed and less emotional, it needs to help its opponents to understand the great capacity for development that independence can bring. Concentrating its efforts on winning over conservative voters with fresh arguments on the likes of currency, for example, is a one-way ticket to another defeat.

As 2014 drifts ever further into folklore, the independence movement must resist dancing to Better Together's ghostly tune. It needs to bring the rest of Scotland with it, not tailor its position to suit a flawed narrative perpetuated by an apathetic majority.

EYES AHEAD

"Don't talk to me of Scotland the Brave, for if we don't fight soon there'll be nothing left to save; or would you rather stand and watch them dig your grave, while you wait for the Tartan Messiah?"

Brian McNeill

It was only really as the final results came in, during the early hours of 19 September 2014, that I finally accepted the inevitable: Scotland had voted against its own independence, and that culmination of years of hope, energy and positivity was snuffed out, literally overnight.

The days that followed the referendum saw Scotland plunged into a collective state of depression. Even the weather was appropriately grey and deflated.

As I walked home in the early morning autumn rain, I tore my Yes badge off and threw it away. Why? Because in that moment, I had ceased to believe in all it represented. That the people best placed to make decisions on Scotland's future were those living here, seemed at once demonstrably untrue. Perhaps Better Together had been right all along; perhaps Scots just didn´t have it in them.

It has always been a somewhat defining trait of Scots that we are suspicious of anyone with ambition, anyone who seeks to diverge from the status quo in any field. Who do they think they are, after all? It's often been noted that ambitious Scots must leave Scotland to realise their potential – history is littered with examples of plucky, ingenious Scots, few of whom achieved greatness here at home.

There are those who'd go further still, arguing that ambitious Scots have long since left the gene pool entirely, leaving behind their more docile brethren in the wake of numerous exoduses, only to be further beaten into submission by a heady dose of Presbyterianism, shite weather and a historical typecasting as wartime cannon fodder.

Scottish culture is cause for embarrassment for huge swathes of Scots, who all too often see it as twee, tacky and nationalistic. Accordingly, Scottish literature, traditional music, Scots and Gaelic language, are not only under-resourced, under-funded and under-exposed, but their active suppression is routine and mainstream. It is a distinctly Scottish pastime to revel in the collective disdain of our own cultural heritage. The writer and broadcaster Billy Kay put it best, describing his childhood in Ayrshire, where he was "given a prize by the Burns Federation one day a year for reciting Rabbie's poetry – and given the belt the other 364 days for speaking his guid Scots tongue."[37]

But 2014 was different, or at least it seemed different. That referendum was about Scottish independence, but in many respects it was really a battle for the soul of Scotland. For the first time in centuries, that don´t-get-above-yersel' attitude seemed to have receded, perhaps even into the minority. Of course, there were a great many moving parts to the independence referendum of 2014, but a palpable sense of hope and community really stemmed from a shared sense that Scots were beginning to shake off their sense of inferiority. That belief in ourselves – but most importantly, in each other – created the nightmare scenario, feared by powerful elites since time immemorial: *ordinary people working together.*

Brian McNeill wrote the song 'No Gods and Precious Few Heroes' during the 1980s, and released it during the 1990s. An angry song about Scotland's romanticised past, and its seeming inability to work together to bring about the change it needs, seems more relevant than ever, in this post-2014 Scotland:

> So don't talk to me about Scotland the Brave
> If we don't fight soon there'll be nothing left to save
> Or would you rather stand and watch them dig your grave
> While you wait for the Tartan Messiah?
> He'll lead us to the Promised Land wi' laughter in his eye
> We'll all off the oil and the whisky by and by
> Free heavy beer! Pie suppers in the sky!
> Will we never have the sense to learn?
>
> *Brian McNeill*

The strange paralysis that's gripped Scotland in the wake of 2014 is epitomised in these lines. Too many now believe that until we have achieved independence, there is no space for new ideas; we must simply wait patiently for our contemporary "Tartan Messiah" to fire the starting gun on another referendum.

The post-2014 independence movement has been emboldened by the continued influence of the SNP, and sections of it have become extremely protective of that dominance. On the surface, it may sound somewhat counter-intuitive, but if one thing might undo the independence juggernaut, it could be an over-reliance on the SNP.

The SNP has, of course, worked towards the goal of independence since its inception, and for the best part of a century it did so alone and against the tide of public opinion. But what made the referendum of 2014 possible was a realisation that the movement had grown into something more than a single political party, that it had evolved into something much bigger, it had come of age.

The opponents of Yes fought tooth and nail throughout the 2014 campaign to suppress anything that presented the Yes movement as anything greater than the Scottish National Party. Consequently, many unionists will still look at you with confusion when you suggest otherwise.

As I've discussed in detail throughout this book, that impression of the Yes campaign as a single party obsession ultimately won out, and it's not unrealistic to suggest that it may have cost 5 per cent of the vote.

The partisan narrative was pushed by a media that was inexperienced in covering major political events outside of elections, yet it was aided greatly by the SNP too. In many ways, the moment Alex Salmond agreed to debate Alistair Darling in a string of televised debates he cemented the Yes campaign's legacy as an SNP one – which it most certainly was not.

Has the independence movement learned that lesson though? On the surface it would seem not to have. The post-2014 campaign now looks more SNP-dominated than ever before. Alex Salmond's leadership was replaced with that of Nicola Sturgeon, but the party's perceived ownership over independence is now more embedded than it ever was.

Of course, it's perfectly logical for the disillusioned Yes vote to have transferred itself to the dominant independence-supporting party, and for those keen to see a second referendum sooner, rather than later, an SNP government is a patent necessity. But whether a sooner-rather-than-later approach to a second referendum is the most sensible approach is difficult to say.

*   *   *

Scotland's future is uncertain, on that at least we can all agree. There is a broad consensus now that independence is all but inevitable – indeed, a 2015 Panelbase poll[38] showed over two-thirds of Scots believed it would happen before 2045.

On the morning of 24 June 2016, it was clear that the independence movement had shifted into a new chapter. The Brexit vote meant that the campaign of 2014 had passed quickly and unceremoniously into the annals of history, as independence suddenly became about something very different, and something far more pressing.

The diplomatic wrangling and careful planning required to keep Scotland inside the European Union had the potential to place the Scottish government at the forefront of negotiations. Unlike in 2014, where they were merely pushing a point of principle, they now found themselves defending Scotland in a far more urgent and existential sense.

Despite the guile and expertise the Scottish government undoubtedly has at its fingertips, though, the decision Scotland made in 2014 renders it powerless to intervene and effect any real change without the good grace of a sympathetic UK government; and there is no tactical advantage whatsoever to any unionist UK government in demonstrating any such cooperation.

With all that in mind, those of us who wish to see

Scotland independent must be prepared to weather some hard years. We must brace ourselves for the prospect that it might not happen quickly, and when it does happen, it won't be a straight re-run of 2014.

As we face down years – possibly decades – of controversy, we'll have to pull together, united behind a single banner, but at the same time nurturing the diversity that made the Yes movement so successful. We can't lose sight of who we are in the name of a single moment in history – after all, that single moment is worth nothing if we've homogenised behind a shadow of what made it worthwhile in the first place.

The SNP cannot do this alone. It – just like the wider movement – needs similarly independence-minded, yet otherwise politically diverse minds, too.

The future of the independence movement, and the key to its success will require, as it did in 2014, more than one political party – namely the Greens and the Socialists and, who knows, maybe even support from within the dwindling ranks of Scottish Labour: stranger things have happened.

There is nothing wrong with believing in a party – indeed, there's nothing wrong with wanting others to believe in it too, but we must remember that for as long as independence belongs to a single political party, it cannot belong to the whole of Scotland.

Imagine a future campaign for a Yes vote in which any attempt to paint it as a single party issue would be impossible: a genuine cross-party movement – divided on many things, but united in its shared desire for an independent Scotland. Now imagine how much more attractive a prospectus that would be to those people who – rightly or wrongly – didn't particularly object to the idea of independence, but who harboured a deep mistrust of the SNP.

It is a well-meaning but extremely flawed argument

that says we should keep the flame of 2014 burning, and the Yes campaign preserved in aspic until the next referendum.

The strength of the 2014 Yes campaign was its get-up-and-go, its ability to fundamentally look beyond the process and symbolism of independence, and begin planning that next chapter in Scotland's story with real purpose. The strength of that campaign was built on its diversity; it disagreed on many things, but was united behind one cause. That strategy is sustainable – indeed powerful – during a two-year campaign, but to try and keep it up indefinitely is a recipe for disaster.

As the civil rights activist Audre Lorde once said: "It is not our differences that divide us. It is our inability to recognise, accept, and celebrate those differences." It's not merely possible to express solidarity with fellow independistas from opposite ends of the political spectrum and parties of every hue, it's *necessary* if Scotland is to realise its future as an independent country.

*   *   *

He who fails to learn from history is doomed to repeat it. Throughout the 2014 referendum, the Yes campaign found itself – for better or worse – dancing to the tune of the SNP who, in turn, found themselves dancing to the tune of the Better Together campaign. They tacitly handed their opponents the mantle of economic literacy by bending over backwards to conduct a debate on their opponent's terms. The media was thus able to present the referendum as one whose fate would rise and fall on the likelihood of something as mind-numbingly straightforward as a currency union.

Because of that, the inspiring scenes from packed town hall meetings taking place every night, in every corner of Scotland, never made it to our television screens, never found their way into the newspapers and – crucially – never reached the people they needed to reach.

Post-2014 polling on independence is perhaps the most effective illustration of the uneasy place in which Scotland's independence movement finds itself. We can argue about why support doesn't seem to have moved much – even in the face of a Conservative majority in Westminster, a deeply unpopular Brexit vote, even a Donald Trump Presidency in the US – but one thing we can agree on, is that whatever strategy we've been taking since 2014, it patently hasn't been working. If we don't face up to that fact, then aren't we just careering headlong towards yet another glorious Scottish defeat?

*   *   *

To say that Scots weren't convinced by the arguments for independence is to tell only a part of the story, as the vast majority of Scots simply weren't privy to those arguments. The Better Together campaign skilfully distracted us all, ensuring that we spent the majority of our time effectively banging our heads against a brick wall with nonsensical, often contradictory economic bluster, so that the real arguments – which, lest we forget, inspired almost half of the population – simply didn't get a look-in.

2014 was fun, it was exciting and – despite what the critics say – it brought entire communities together in a spirit unrivalled in most people's lifetimes. It was engaging, it was stimulating, it was positive and it was life changing. But – and this part is crucial – *we lost.*

That an independence referendum only comes along

once in a generation is a logical observation – the 2014 generation came close, but ultimately blew it. But that generation's blood, sweat and tears, its successes, its failures, will form the foundations for the next independence generation.

Scotland will be an independent country one day, that much we know for sure – and we know it to be true by the grit, determination and diversity of the independence movement. That future, however, is still premised on a great deal of hard work, and it won't happen of its own accord. The perseverance and the defeats – many of which may still lie ahead – are merely steps along the road, but Scotland, when she finally wins her independence, will be all the better for that journey.

REFERENCES

(1) Iain Gray – 2010 Speech to Labour Party Conference – UKPOL. 2017. Iain Gray – 2010 Speech to Labour Party Conference – UKPOL. [ONLINE] Available at: http://www.ukpol.co.uk/uncategorized/iain-gray-2010-speech-to-labour-party-conference/. [Accessed 31 January 2017].

(2) HeraldScotland. 2017. Why the fight for independence has left Yes Scotland behind (From HeraldScotland). [ONLINE] Available at: http://www.heraldscotland.com/news/13156457.Why_the_fight_for_independence_has_left_Yes_Scotland_behind/. [Accessed 31 January 2017].

(3) The GuardianNigel Farage flees barrage of abuse from Edinburgh protesters https://www.theguardian.com/politics/2013/may/16/nigel-farage-edinburgh-protesters-van

(4) Scotland Yet: A film about independence, 2014. [DVD] Jack Foster, Scotland: Rough Justice Films.

(5) No Scotland. 2017. Launch of the Better Together campaign – No Scotland. [ONLINE] Available at: https://noscotland.net/2012/06/26/launch-of-the-better-together-campaign/. [Accessed 31 January 2017].

(6) BBC News. 2017. Scottish independence: Pensions 'secure' post-Yes, says UK minister - BBC News. [ONLINE] Available at: http://www.bbc.co.uk/news/uk-scotland-scotland-politics-27309215. [Accessed 31 January 2017].

(7) BBC News. 2017. Bank of England gives 'reassurance' on Scottish independence vote - BBC News. [ONLINE] Available at: http://www.bbc.co.uk/news/business-28777246. [Accessed 31 January 2017].

(8) C'mon Scotland. 2017. C'mon Scotland. [ONLINE] Available at: http://www.cmonscotland.org/single-post/2014/02/11/Currency. [Accessed 31 January 2017].

(9) Sky News. 2017. Scottish Referendum: Leaders Clash In TV Debate. [ONLINE] Available at: http://news.sky.com/story/scottish-referendum-leaders-clash-in-tv-debate-10394117. [Accessed 31 January 2017].

(10) BBC News. 2017. Scottish independence: Salmond denies lying over EU advice - BBC News. [ONLINE] Available at: http://www.bbc.co.uk/news/uk-scotland-scotland-politics-20042069. [Accessed 31 January 2017].

(11) STV News. 2017. North Sea oil and gas revenues projected to nosedive by 2040. [ONLINE] Available at: https://stv.tv/news/politics/233231-north-sea-oil-and-gas-revenues-projected-to-nosedive-by-2040/. [Accessed 31 January 2017].

(12) BBC News. 2017. BBC One - The Andrew Marr Show, 24/01/2016. [ONLINE] Available at: http://www.bbc.co.uk/programmes/b06zc01f. [Accessed 31 January 2017].

(13) Better Together's 500 Questions parodied online - The Scotsman. 2017. Better Together's 500 Questions parodied online - The Scotsman. [ONLINE] Available at: http://www.scotsman.com/news/politics/better-together-s-500-questions-parodied-online-1-2921931. [Accessed 31 January 2017].

(14) Sarah Smith on fronting the BBC's Scotland 2014 show - The Scotsman. 2017. Sarah Smith on fronting the BBC's Scotland 2014 show - The Scotsman. [ONLINE] Available at: http://www.scotsman.com/lifestyle/culture/tv-radio/sarah-smith-on-fronting-the-bbc-s-scotland-2014-show-1-3421848. [Accessed 31 Jan, 2017].

(15) The Guardian. 2017. BBC's Nick Robinson attacks 'bullying' over Scottish referendum coverage | Media | The Guardian. [ONLINE] Available at: https://www.theguardian.com/media/2015/aug/21/bbc-nick-robinson-bullying-scottish-referendum-alex-salmond. [Accessed 31 January 2017].

(16) Mail Online. 2017. Cybernats unmasked: Meet the footsoldiers of pro-Scottish independence 'army' whose online poison shames the Nationalists | Daily Mail Online. [ONLINE] Available at: http://www.dailymail.co.uk/news/article-2545901/Cybernats-unmasked-Meet-footsoldiers-pro-Scottish-independence-army-online-poison-shames-Nationalists.html. [Accessed 31 January 2017].

(17) RT International. 2017. BBC accused of anti-independence bias after editing out Salmond's reply to 'bank exodus' question — RT UK. [ONLINE] Available at: https://www.rt.com/uk/187344-bbc-scottish-independence-bias/. [Accessed 31 January 2017].

(18) Christopher Silver, 2015. Demanding Democracy: The Case for a Scottish Media. Edition. Word Power Books.

(19) The Guardian. 2017. CBI backs no vote in Scottish independence referendum | Politics | The Guardian. [ONLINE] Available at: https://www.theguardian.com/politics/2014/apr/18/cbi-backs-no-vote-scottish-independence-referendum. [Accessed 31 January 2017].

(20) Businesses protest after CBI announces decision to back No campaign. 2017. Businesses protest after CBI announces decision to back No campaign. [ONLINE] Available at: https://stv.tv/amp/272211-businesses-protest-after-cbi-announces-decision-to-back-no-campaign/. [Accessed 31 January 2017].

(21) Barrhead Travel director defends anti-Yes memo - The Scotsman. 2017. Barrhead Travel director defends anti-Yes memo - The Scotsman. [ONLINE] Available at: http://www.scotsman.com/news/politics/barrhead-travel-director-defends-anti-yes-memo-1-3359505. [Accessed 31 January 2017].

(22) Wings Over Scotland. 2017. Wings Over Scotland | Straight from the source. [ONLINE] Available at: http://wingsoverscotland.com/straight-from-the-source/. [Accessed 31 January 2017].

(23) Murray Foote. 2017. Johann Lamont resigns as Scottish Labour leader: Some of my colleagues are dinosaurs, they don't see that things have changed - Daily Record. [ONLINE] Available at: http://www.dailyrecord.co.uk/news/politics/johann-lamont-resigns-scottish-labour-4502765. [Accessed 31 January 2017].

(24) Keir Mudie. 2017. Gordon Brown Scottish referendum speech: Read full transcript of the former Prime Minister's passionate 'No' plea - Mirror Online. [ONLINE] Available at: http://www.mirror.co.uk/news/uk-news/gordon-brown-scottish-referendum-speech-4276089. [Accessed 31 January 2017].

(25) The Independent. 2017. Scottish independence: Listen to George Galloway's stirring speech in defence of the Union | The Independent. [ONLINE] Available at: http://www.independent.co.uk/news/uk/politics/scottish-independence-george-galloway-s-stirring-speech-in-defence-of-the-union-9566418.html. [Accessed 31 January 2017].

(26) How Scotland voted, and why - Lord Ashcroft Polls. 2017. How Scotland voted, and why - Lord Ashcroft Polls. [ONLINE] Available at: http://lordashcroftpolls.com/2014/09/scotland-voted/. [Accessed 31 January 2017].

(27) Internet Access - Households and Individuals - Office for National Statistics. 2017. Internet Access - Households and Individuals - Office for National Statistics. [ONLINE] Available at: https://www.ons.gov.uk/peoplepopulationandcommunity/householdcharacteristics/homeinternetandsocialmediausage/bulletins/internetaccesshouseholdsandindividuals/2015-08-06. [Accessed 31 January 2017].

(28) Ofcom. 2017. Adults' media use and attitudes - Ofcom. [ONLINE] Available at: https://www.ofcom.org.uk/research-and-data/media-literacy-research/adults-media-use-and-attitudes. [Accessed 31 January 2017].

(29) BBC News. 2017. Scottish independence: Jim Murphy suspends campaign tour - BBC News. [ONLINE] Available at: http://www.bbc.co.uk/news/uk-scotland-scotland-politics-28986714. [Accessed 31 January 2017].

(30) Wings Over Scotland. 2017. Wings Over Scotland | Playing with fire. [ONLINE] Available at: http://wingsoverscotland.com/playing-with-fire/. [Accessed 31 January 2017].

(31) The Independent. 2017. Scottish independence: Nationalism is a dangerous political philosophy. I am Scottish and I am British. | The Independent. [ONLINE] Available at: http://www.independent.co.uk/voices/comment/scottish-independence-nationalism-is-a-dangerous-political-philosophy-i-am-scottish-and-i-am-british-9741085.html. [Accessed 31 January 2017].

(32) Scottish independence: Barrowman backs No campaign - The Scotsman. 2017. Scottish independence: Barrowman backs No campaign - The Scotsman. [ONLINE] Available at: http://www.scotsman.com/news/politics/scottish-independence-barrowman-backs-no-campaign-1-3281505. [Accessed 31 January 2017].

(33) STV News. 2017. Essay: Stephen Daisley on the SNP and the politics of nationalism. [ONLINE] Available at: https://stv.tv/news/politics/1322184-essay-stephen-daisley-on-the-snp-and-the-politics-of-nationalism/. [Accessed 01 February 2017].

(34) Mail Online. 2017. Savage racism turning Scotland into a no-go zone for the English | Daily Mail Online. [ONLINE] Available at: http://www.dailymail.co.uk/news/article-2745565/Savage-racism-turning-Scotland-no-zone-English.html. [Accessed 31 January 2017].

(35) BuzzFeed. 2017. Better Together Campaign Chief: We Would Have Struggled To Win Without 'Scaremongering' - BuzzFeed News. [ONLINE] Available at: https://www.buzzfeed.com/sirajdatoo/better-together-campaign-chief-we-would-have-struggled-to-wi?utm_term=.fgVLxxgZq#.ii3oRRxym. [Accessed 31 January 2017].

(36) Reuters. 2017. Former NATO chief warns Scottish independence would be 'cataclysmic' | Reuters. [ONLINE] Available at: http://www.reuters.com/article/us-scotland-independence-idUSBREA370YK20140408. [Accessed 31 January 2017].

(37) Scotsman.com. (2018). Billy Kay: A masterpiece that strikes fear and excitement, an incomparable epic tale all Scots can be proud of. [online] Available at: https://www.scotsman.com/lifestyle/culture/books/billy-kay-a-masterpiece-that-strikes-fear-and-excitement-an-incomparable-epic-tale-all-scots-can-be-proud-of-1-2072068 [Accessed 16 Mar. 2018].

(38) Scottish independence 'inevitable by 2045' - poll - The Scotsman. 2017. Scottish independence 'inevitable by 2045' - poll - The Scotsman. [ONLINE] Available at: http://www.scotsman.com/news/politics/scottish-independence-inevitable-by-2045-poll-1-3885463. [Accessed 12 May 2017].

Printed in Great Britain
by Amazon